CB

Ple·

# Last Letters
## to
# Loved Ones

# Last Letters to Loved Ones

## Rose Rouse

metro

Published by Metro Publishing
an imprint of John Blake Publishing Ltd,
3 Bramber Court, 2 Bramber Road,
London W14 9PB, England

www.blake.co.uk

First published in hardback in 2008

ISBN: 978-1-84454-576-6

British Library Cataloguing-in-Publication Data:

A catalogue record for this book is available from the British Library.

Design by www.envydesign.co.uk

Printed in the UK by CPI William Clowes Beccles NR34 7TL

1 3 5 7 9 10 8 6 4 2

Papers used by John Blake Publishing are natural, recyclable products
made from wood grown in sustainable forests. The manufacturing processes
conform to the environmental regulations of the country of origin.

Every attempt has been made to contact the relevant copyright-holders,
but some were unobtainable. We would be grateful if the appropriate
people could contact us.

For my father, an inveterate letter writer
who didn't write a last letter.

She wrote me a letter after her death,
and I remember a kind of happy light
as I sat by the rose tree
on her old bench by the back door
so surprised to receive it
wondering what she would say
looking up before I could open it
and laughing to myself in silent expectation.

*Farewell Letter*, David Whyte

## Acknowledgements

Thanks to Wensley Clarkson for suggesting the idea for this book to me. Also, thanks to the archivists at the Imperial War Museum for helping me find the right World War I and World War II collections; thanks also to the archivists at the Wellcome Trust Library; and, finally, huge thanks to those trusting individuals who have allowed me to publish last letters from their loved ones. Wise words from Rod Suddaby, Phillip Hodson and Malcolm Stern were appreciated.

# Contents

*Introduction*

Over the summer of 2007, I found myself inhabiting a new world. It was the deeply personal and often heartbreakingly moving world of last letters to loved ones.

In my research, I pondered who would write such letters, and quickly realised that soldiers, the fatally ill, the suicidal and prisoners about to be executed all had an increased impetus to write such a letter, although I have also included a few wartime last letters that are incidental in order to illustrate the differences in tone and thought when these letters are not deliberately written as their last ones. I have also added a final chapter of famous last letters because these possess their own fascination, whether it be the narcissistic musings of Nirvana lead singer Kurt Cobain before he killed himself, or writer Hunter S Thompson's wry wit before he put a shotgun to his temple.

In order to find these last letters, I wrote to editors of local newspapers asking readers to get in touch with me if they had such letters that they were willing to have published; I spent afternoons immersed in wartime letter collections at the Imperial War Museum and the Wellcome Trust

Library, and I explored the endless possibilities on the Internet. All avenues threw up different treasures.

At times, I was startled when I found recent last letters from young soldiers – 19- and 20-year-olds – who had died in Iraq or Afghanistan, because their words seemed so casual and unknowing about war, yet they expressed their love so clearly. At other times, I was amazed at the eagerness of World War II soldiers to tell their loved ones how fiercely proud they were to be serving their country and presumably also to save their families some grief. I was always moved by World War I soldiers' determination and fortitude in appalling conditions. All these wartime last letters were written with a tremendous generosity of spirit.

The letters of the fatally ill were, for me, the most affecting in the book. Often, young mothers – in their 30s – dying of cancer grasp this opportunity to tell their children and partners just how much they are loved and will be missed. They are unfailingly written with immense courage. The certainty of their deaths seems to grip their pens and caress the page in their precious last words.

Suicide notes are different. Mostly, the writers of these notes are desperate and sometimes angry. Whereas the fatally ill have often come to terms with their imminent death, the suicidal are sometimes motivated by revenge as well as hopelessness. Sometimes, they tell their families not to blame themselves; at other times, they say exactly the opposite.

Equally, last statements from prisoners soon to be executed can err on the side of economy with the truth. Sometimes, however, they are simply seeking forgiveness, while at other times they are still trying to convince others that they are innocent. Whatever the motivation, all these last letters are interesting for what they leave out, as well as what they put in.

It is impossible to avoid the potency of a last letter. To the loved ones, this letter is a tangible vestige of their partner or child or friend. This letter is the final proof that the dead person and their love existed. The last letter gives the recipient something to hold on to, when his or her emotional universe may be collapsing. It represents certainty in an otherwise uncertain existence.

In editing these last letters, I decided to mix

contemporary and historical letters together, hoping that the juxtaposition will throw up questions. I have also included last letters from other nationalities as well as the British. Through them, we now have insights into what members of the Russian resistance went through during World War II; or the honour and pride involved in a kamikaze pilot's view of the world; or the extreme reasons for killing themselves explained in anonymous German suicide notes; or what US prisoners said recently just before they were executed. All of these perspectives paint a bigger and more complicated global picture, which is one we, as a society, still need to understand more fully.

Finally, I have discovered what a sacred place the last letter occupies within the healing of a grieving heart. It definitely made me want to write one before I depart.

Please note, I have allowed some idiosyncracies, mis-spellings and dialect features to remain in the letters, trying to retain the original voice of the writer wherever possible, except where the grammar or syntax leads to confusion or obvious error.

# 1

## Iraq and Afghanistan

Gunner Lee Thornton, 22 years old, from Blackpool was fatally shot after volunteering to take part in a dangerous patrol north of Basra in Iraq on 7 September 2006. His close friend, Corporal Stephen Wright, was killed by a roadside bomb on the same patrol the day before. Lee was in the 12th Regiment Royal Artillery and he was the 118th British soldier to be killed in Iraq and the third from his unit to be killed in three days.

Following an unofficial army tradition, which goes back to World War I in the UK, Lee had written a last letter to his fiancée, 21-year-old Helen O'Pray, just in case he did not return. It was a tenderly handwritten letter which he hoped would never be opened. Lee had secretly entrusted it to her parents when he had visited her home for her 21st birthday. The couple were due to marry in 2008 after he'd completed his second tour of Iraq. Tragically, that marriage was never to be.

Helen said at the time, 'I cannot put into words how I feel about losing Lee. He was my life and I'll never forget him. There are no words that can describe how I felt when I read the letter for the first time. I love him so much. He was kind, generous and everything you would want in a man. I miss him dearly and this letter just shows how much I meant to him.'

Helen and his parents were at his side at a military hospital in Germany when he died. The doctors tried hard to save him but could not. He was killed by a single shot. His father, Mick, said afterwards, 'He's an absolute hero. Everyone who met Lee knew they were meeting someone special. We will never forget him or what he achieved.'

This is the incredibly passionate last love letter that Lee wrote to Helen. It is poignant how direct he is about his love for her. It's as if being in a war zone, and therefore facing death, enabled him to articulate feelings he may never have been able to express in a face-to-face encounter.


*Hi babe,*

*I don't know why I am writing this because I really hope that this letter never gets to you, because if it does that means I am dead. It also means I never had time to show you just how much I really did love you.*

*You have shown me what love is and what it*

feels like to be loved. Every time you kissed me and our lips touched so softly I could feel it. I got the same magical feeling as our first kiss. I would feel it when our hearts get so close they are beating as one. You are the beat of my heart, the soul in my body; you are me because without you I am nothing. I love you, Helen, you are my girlfriend, my fiancée and my best friend.

You are the person I know I could turn to when I needed help … you are the person I looked at when I needed to smile and you are the person I went to when I needed a hug. When I am away it is like I have left my soul at your side. You have shown me so much while you have been in my life that if I lost you I could not live. You have shown me how to live and you have shown me how to be truly happy. I want you to know that every time I smile that you have put it there. You make me smile when others can't, you make me feel warm when I am cold.

You have shown me so much love and so much more. I want you to know how much you mean to me. You are my whole world and I love you with all my heart, you are my happiness.

There is no sea or ocean that could stop my love for you. It is the biggest thing I have ever had.

When I say I love I am trying to say … that you make me feel warm and great about myself, you make me smile and laugh every day; you make time to talk to me and listen to what I have to say. I know God put me and you on this earth to find each other, fall in love and show the rest of the world what true love really is.

I know this is going to sound sad but every night I spent away I had a photo of you on my headboard. Each night I would go to bed, kiss my fingers then touch your face. I put the photo over my bed so you could look over me as I slept. Well, now it is my turn to look over you as you sleep and keep you safe in your dreams.

I will always be looking over you to make sure you're safe. Helen, I want to say something and I mean this more than I ever did before. You were the love of my life, the girl of my dreams.

Just because I have passed away does not mean I am not with you. I'll always be there looking over you keeping you safe.

So whenever you feel lonely, just close your eyes and I'll be there right by your side. I really did love you with all I had, you were everything to me.

*Never forget that, and never forget I will*
*always be looking over you. I love you, you are*
*my soulmate.*

*Love always and for ever,*
*Lee*

*       ★       ★       ★*

Neil Downes, 20, a guardsman from Droylsden
near Manchester, joined the army when he was
just 17. He'd already completed a posting in
Basra, and had been in Afghanistan for 12 weeks.
Neil was on patrol with Afghan troops in an
operation to widen and deepen irrigation ditches
when his truck hit a landmine, which exploded.
He was killed on 9 June 2007 while serving with
the 1st Battalion of the Grenadier Guards; four of
his comrades were injured. Neil was the 60th
British soldier to die in Afghanistan since 2001.

He had written a surprisingly casual-sounding
last letter to his girlfriend, 19-year-old Jane Little, a
trainee business travel consultant who had met him
in her hometown, Aldershot, seven months earlier.
But the tone probably originates from his naïveté –
in other words, he just couldn't imagine actually
dying. Neil had told his Major that he was thinking

7

*Neil Downes*

of asking her to marry him. When she found out after he'd been killed, she declared that she would have definitely become his wife if he'd asked her.

He also wrote another last letter to his parents, Sheryl and Ronnie, that was only to be opened in the event of his death. In that letter, he wrote, 'Please do not be mad at what has happened. I did what I had to do and serving the British Army was it.'

His mother said, 'We are very proud that he served as a soldier. We wouldn't have stood in his way.'

Neil's last letter to Jane is all the more touching because it seems to be from a 20-year-old soldier who is so innocent on the subject of his own mortality and the terrible effects of war. It's almost shockingly light-hearted, filled with little jokes. By writing it, he is fulfilling a duty, but his naïveté has yet to be punctured.

However, the unbelievable did happen. Jane receives some small comfort in this letter. 'It is hard to read the letter but it does help,' she has said. 'I will never forget him.' She also said, 'He was the perfect boyfriend. I am immensely proud of him and all he did.'

*Hey beautiful,*

*I'm sorry I had to put you through all this, darling. I'm truly sorry.*

*Just thought I'll leave you with a last few words.*

*All I wanna say is how much I loved you, and cared for you. You are the apple of my eye, and I will be watching over you always.*

*Mary-Jane, Ian, Tom, Craig, Lee, thank you all for accepting me in to be able to care for your daughter/sister. I will not forget how nice you have been to me!*

*Bet now my bloody lottery numbers will come up! Ha ha.*

*Jane, I hope you have a wonderful and fulfilling life! Get married, Have children, etc!*

*I will love you forever and will see you again when you're old and wrinkly!*

*I have told my parents to leave you some money out of my insurance so have fun bbz!*

*Ok… gonna go now, beautiful.*

*Love you forever…*

*Neil*

★   ★   ★

Private Leon Spicer, 26 years old, from Tamworth in Staffordshire, was killed by a roadside bomb in Iraq during May 2005, just one week before he was due to leave the country. He had written a heart-wrenching last letter to his parents only to be opened in the event of his death. Despite being badly spelled, it is a powerfully emotive letter.

He manages to express very tender love for his parents and family, which he may not have been able to do in person. At least this offers his loved ones some solace.

His mother Bridie has said, 'It was so sad but, at the same time, such a comfort. It was lovely to know there was so much love there.'

*Dear Mum and Dad,*

*If u'r reading this I've gone somewhere that all of you haven't. Don't cry cos if u do, I'll have a word with GOD and tell him not to let you all in.*

*Right then, I new what could happen to me but it was my job, and I wanted to do it. Remember, I LOVE YOU ALL (u and dad more) ONLY JOKEING! Gerard's the best brother any brother could ask four and as 4 NINA, my only sister, I loved her to bits.*

*Leon Spicer*

*So stop crying, cos I am as I write this.*

*I've had the BEST LIFE out of any one in the whole world. Right then, mom what can I say about u? If I wanted to say everything I would need about 10 million note books but I can put it into 5 words – THE BEST MOM IN THE WORLD!*

*PS I need to count cos I do believe there where six words*

*Now DAD u'r the BEST DAD IN THE WORLD and I hope u've known it. I love u so much, we had everything in comen, but I think I took scouting too far (ie I JOINED THE ARMY) between u and me, we were the only ones that could survive in the woods.*

*I loved everything that u done and wanted to do it from camping to being a leader.*

*RIGHT I'm going to bed to tell Grandmar how much I love her, she's the best in the world and tell to look after Edey.*

*SEE YOU ALL SOON. I'LL BE THERE WAITING FOUR YOU ALL.*

*Lots of LOVE*
*LEON xxx*

★   ★   ★

*Ben Hyde*

*Ben Hyde*

Lance Corporal Ben Hyde, 23 years old, from Northallerton in North Yorkshire, was a military policeman who was killed by a mob at Majar al-Kabir, near Basra, in July 2003. Ben's hospital- porter dad, John, said he was proud of the bravery shown by his son and his comrades during their last moments when a gang of Iraqi insurgents executed them inside a police station.

Ben was buried with full military honours and his coffin was draped with the Union flag, red beret, white belt and regimental bayonet. His last letter was read out by the padre Jonathan Ball and hundreds of mourners lined the streets and listened to Ben's brave, generous last words to his parents. This is a mature last letter which even mentions forgiveness, showing that Ben is able to have a wider perspective.

15

Dear Mum and Dad

If you are reading this, then you will know I won't be coming home. I am up in the stars now looking down on you making sure that you are safe.

I am sorry for all the times I have been a pain but I know the good times outweighed the bad tenfold.

Thank you for being the best parents anyone could ever have wished for and you gave me everything I could ever have wanted and more.

You have both got long lives ahead of you yet so make sure you make use of every second you have because sitting here writing this now I know just how precious time is.

Tell the rest of the family I was thinking of them and make sure they all take care.

Forgiveness is something every body deserves because one day, it may be too late.

Remember that every time you are thinking of me, I am thinking of you too. Look after yourselves,

All my love,

Ben

★   ★   ★

Anthony Butterfield, a 19-year-old marine, was from California, and he joined up straight after school. He was one of four marines who were killed when a suicide bomber caused a propane truck to explode in Rawah, Iraq, on 2 July 2006. He'd been in Iraq for four months.

He wrote this last letter to his family, and the reader can't help but be aware of how young the writer is, and how little of life he has actually experienced. That is the underlying tragedy. Somehow, his everyday home memories emphasise how unsafe his everyday military life was. One of his fellow marines described afterwards how much he had been looking forward to seeing his mother again. Of course, tragically, he never did.

*Hi Mom, Dad, Britney, Jeremy, and Bailey,*

*If your getting this letter then I'm sure you've already heard. I'm so sorry. But know that I am safe now. I'm with God watching over you. I'll always be with you all. You'll know when I'm around because you'll feel me. I wanna tell you all some special memories I'll always hold on too.*

*Staying up late with you, mom, watching the*

*Anthony Butterfield*

food channel while you rub my back, or when I was little and you'd always get me a glass of chocolate milk with a lid and a straw.

With you, Dad, going out on the sidecar and driving to volleyball tournaments, just you and me.

Britney when you used to drop me off at school and I thought I was so cool cause all my friends got rides from there parents. You were always like a second mom to me Brit, trying to hold my hand crossing the street.

Jeremy you and me always building cool ass stuff. A wagon with an engine, a bicycle with an engine, and a bicycle sidecar. Or just chillin in the backyard riding motorcycles for hours.

Bailey, remember all those late nights when you'd come into my room and we'd just talk. And just hangin out with my little sister.

I always loved going to the beach house as a family and spending time with each other constantly smiling playing in the sand. I thank god every day for blessing me with such an amazing family. You all mean the world to me. I hope I've made you all proud. I love you all with all of my heart and please don't be sad, just know

*that I made it to heaven before you and will see
you all again.*

*Your loving son/brother,*
*Anthony Edward Butterfield*

★   ★   ★

Thirty-two-year-old Glen Arnold, a Canadian
corporal, was killed by a suicide bomber during
a foot patrol in the Panjumi district of
Afghanistan.

The night before he left for Afghanistan, he
sent a farewell email to his entire family – his
parents, his wife, his four children, his sister and
his three brothers. He wanted to make sure he
had said goodbye in case he died. At the time, his
nine-year-old nephew Jackson was in hospital
with severe burns.

Glen had been in the armed forces for 14 years
and was a medical technician. He'd served in
war-torn Sri Lanka and Bosnia-Herzegovina,
but, sadly, he didn't survive Afghanistan.

His last email is full of kindness and generosity
of spirit; it's a testament to Glen's loving nature.
As he's older than many of the soldiers whose
letters have been published in this collection,

there is a noticeable maturity in his attitude towards life and his family. He wants to leave them words that have meaning and that will, in some way, take care of them. He leaves them with the warmth and depth of his feeling for them.

*It's been a long time in coming but, to many, including myself, not long enough. I have only hours before it is time to leave. During my time away, I have a few short words for some. Dean, Jackson and Bailey... I know that the three of you have started on the long road of healing. A tragic accident has occurred and you have found yourselves to be closer than you thought. Dean, you find that your kids love you more than you thought possible, and Bailey and Jackson, you see that Dad will do anything it takes for you. Dean, worry about your family, not me. That is my wish. I love you and am proud of the way you have handled everything so far. You are a man I admire.*

*Mom and Dad... I find myself in a position that is tearing at your soul. You have a son and grandchildren who need you while you have to see your other son separated from his family to go on* a mission many don't understand or support. I can only imagine the agony this causes. You have made the right choice, though, in staying at Dean's side.

Wayne, Lynn and Lance… you find yourselves seeing a brother depart on a mission that has more than its share of tragedy; this is widely public in the media. You question will this happen to your family, a tragic spotlight is no place for anyone to find themselves in. Since it is me leaving, I can't even imagine the position you find yourselves in or the feelings that come with it. Support Dean, he needs your help.

All other family and friends… I know that you will be wondering how I am doing. I will try to send emails out to let you all know every now and again. Pray for my family and hold proud. Mostly pray for Dean, Jackson and Bailey.

Kerry… my wife. I keep you for last not because that is your lot in life but because that is how important you are to me. You mean the world to me and I will never be able to express the appreciation I have for the love and support you have shown me. You have made it possible for me to be with injured family when you could have been selfish and you have never once asked me to *push my career aside although I know at times it hurts you. I pray for the strength to emulate your courage and strength.*

*Jessica…You have made me proud to call you my daughter, I have faith in you and I know that you will succeed in anything you do. You are a talented, bright and a beautiful young lady. Please help your mother while I'm gone and have patience with her emotions in my absence.*

*Katie… I know that you will miss me and I will miss you too. I love you Katie. I don't know how this email will reach you because I don't have your email address that works.*

*Sam… I will miss you, I love you and I will be back.*

*Connor… I hope that you never forget me and that you will always be proud of what I do.*

*Till next time.*

*I love you all,*

*Glen*

\* \* \*

Private William Cushley, a 21-year-old Canadian, was killed in battle with the Taliban in Afghanistan on 3 September 2006.

The morning he left for Afghanistan, his mother Elaine dropped him off at the bus stop. He gave her one last hug and left for Kandahar. She bet him $50 that she would not cry but, as soon as he got on the bus, she lost her bet. Will must have anticipated that this was an extremely dangerous posting, because he left a handwritten last note for his mother just in case he died. If he had lived, she would never have had to open it. Sadly, she read it.

*If you are reading this, I'm sorry, but I will not be coming back home. Thank you for everything you have ever done for me. I really do appreciate it. You were always there for me even when I didn't want you to be. I have one last favour to ask you. In this envelope is two more letters, one for Tasha, one for Brandy. If you could please deliver them to them I would really appreciate it.*

*I just want you to know that I love you and that I fought bravely and did everything I could to come home. Do not weep too much, I will always be with you in heart and spirit. Love always and forever,*
   *Will*
   *PS You can keep the $50! LOL.*

# 2
## World War II

Going back over 60 years to World War II, these soldiers write last letters home that show how much more formal that era was – in every way. The contemporary letters from soldiers who served in Iraq and Afghanistan are much more casual, yet also more intimate, the feelings much more directly expressed. They've often been informed by TV programmes as opposed to books, and they often appear childlike and touchingly innocent. This is not surprising because most of these soldiers are very young.

The last letters written during World War II are often idealistic in their tone, and show soldiers who are unerring in their devotion to serving their country; they are also much more formally written. There is also notably a class difference; the writers of the modern-day letters tend to be working-class boys who've fulfilled their dreams in some way by becoming soldiers, whereas the letters below are mostly written by well-educated, middle-class men who came to World War II at a slightly older age. They were men rather than boys. However, they also see their dedication to duty in a higher realm; this was a period in history when – in Britain, at least – to serve one's country meant a lot more than it does now. The objective was clearer. These soldiers were more committed to the role they were playing in a war that was absolutely necessary.

The Russian, Japanese and Armenian/French last letters add other perspectives to our historical world view. Their priorities may be ideological, although they are all similar in their desire to express love, save their families unnecessary sadness and assure them that they are content with their lot.

★　　★　　★

Captain Jocelyn Nicholls, a 25-year-old from Fulham, was in the No 7 Commando troop serving in the Mediterranean and Far East. He was killed while leading his troop on 11 May 1942, in Burma.

He wrote this last letter to his mother in the event of his death during his military duties. It's obvious that part of the function of this letter is to enable his mother to feel that he knows he is in the right place and doing the right thing, thereby hoping to minimise her grief. There is also the focus on comradeship, and the distinctly

*Captain Jocelyn Nicholls*

patronising 'I expect it's hard for a woman to understand' that it would be hard to imagine being written now. However, it is a touching testament to his devotion to his mother.

*Dear Mother,*

*I am writing this letter in case an emergency should arise, and not in any gloomy spirit, but I don't like leaving things to chance, and to put it bluntly, you will only get this if I get scuffered, and in that event, there are some things I should like to say. I know it's easy for me to say 'don't grieve for me', but I have had a marvellous life in every way, particularly since the war started. I think I have crammed into it more experience and interest than most people who are ten years older than I am.*

*I know it's not the thing to say, but I have loved the war; I have had with me, for nearly two years of it, the finest lot of chaps a man could wish to command. We've been through quite a lot together, and have a mutual respect and comradeship that nothing in this world can break. Together we fear nothing, in this world or the next. I expect it's hard for a woman to understand this; no man could ask more of Life than this.*

*I want to thank you, Mum, for the wonderful Mother you have been to me. There are many times when I am away from you when I think about you, and the way you've slaved and sacrificed yourself for me, and I can't hope to express my gratitude to you for that.*

*I do believe that everything doesn't end here, and that there is an after life…*

*Since I've know Daphne [his girlfriend, presumably] I've had everything, and every happiness that I could ever hope for. If anyone ever died happily, I shall, and the only thing that does worry me is you, and Daphne. And you two are the only people I care about in this world – and in a different way, my men; and what I am trying to say affects you all.*

*So goodbye to you both, and say 'Goodbye' to my man for me, and God bless and keep you all, always.*

*Jocelyn*

★　★　★

Mick Scott was 24 and a prep-school master when World War II started. He'd always dreamed of learning to fly and joined the RAF immediately.

Mick Scott

Having learned in nine months as opposed to the usual two years because he was so gifted, he made his first operational flight on 24 May 1941. Tragically, it was to be his last. He went missing over the North Sea and was never heard of again.

In fact, although Mick loved flying, he hated the idea of war. Listening to music was often his spiritual escape, but so was flying. However, he was also absolutely clear that Nazism was wrong and detested the idea of 'our children having their souls sterilised by Nazi doctrines'. He was committed to fighting against Hitler's ideas. 'The most horrible aspect of Nazism is its system of education, of driving in instead of leading out, and of putting State above all things spiritual.' In fact, it transpired that Mick's plane had been on a special mission. His body was never found.

He had a distinctly spiritual side to his belief system because he was able to write to his sister, Flora, in 1940, 'The thought of coming to a sticky end does not worry me in the least and it ought not to worry you. Life is merely a passing phase in our development, the rest of which is obscure at present, but undoubtedly there, if not in the accepted Christian sense.'

Mick wrote a profoundly affecting last letter to his parents just weeks before his death. He also conveys the liberation that flying represented for him and how it had a transcendent dimension for him. He was fulfilled by the pleasure of flying, and therefore able to contemplate his own end philosophically.

*Dear Mother and Daddy,*

*You now know that you will not be seeing me any more, and perhaps the knowledge is better than the months of uncertainty which you have been through. There are one or two things which I should like you to know, and which I have been too shy to let you know in person.*

*Firstly, let me say how splendid you both have been during this terrible war. Neither of you have shown how hard things must have been, and when peace comes this will serve to knit the family together as it should always have been knit. As a family, we are terrible afraid of showing our feelings, but war has uncovered unsuspected layers of affection beneath the crust of gentlemanly reserve.*

*Secondly, I would like to thank you both for what you have done for me personally. Nothing has been too much trouble, and I have appreciated this to the full, even if I have been unable to show my appreciation.*

*Finally, a word of comfort. You both know how I have hated this war, and dreaded the thought of it all my life. It has, however, done this for me. It has shown me new realms where man is free from earthly restrictions and conventions; where he can be himself playing hide and seek with the clouds, or watching a strangely silent world beneath, rolling quietly on, touched only by vague unsubstantial shadows moving placidly but unrelenting across its surface. So please don't pity me for the price I have had to pay for this experience. This price is incalculable, but it may just as well be incalculably small as incalculably large, so why worry?*

*There is only one thing to add. Good luck to you all.*

\* \* \*

This next letter moves us geographically to the Soviet Union during World War II. Leonid Silin joined the army (he hid his medical records which showed that he had a weak heart) when the war started. He was married to Anna and had two young sons, Lenya and Gennady. These were difficult years for the Soviet Union – three months of war had seen the Germans getting halfway across the Ukraine. As a consequence, Leonid's unit were forced to beat a retreat in 1941 and a large group of badly wounded soldiers were cut off in a village, where the wounded (including Leonid) were hiding out in local barns.

On one occasion, they could hear German voices outside the barns and knew that the Nazis would set fire to them if they knew who was inside. Leonid, who had grown up among German families in the Ukraine, went out and implored the Germans to hold their fire in faultless German. They were so surprised that they agreed, and Leonid was taken to their headquarters.

Once there, Leonid convinced them he was a German sympathiser with the sole aim of requesting to organise a hospital for his wounded comrades. He also pretended to be a Soviet medical doctor. The Germans were impressed and gave him permission, and he created what was to be known as Leonid's Ukrainian hospital. The Germans refused to allow any wounded to go who were Soviet officers, communists, Jews or Russians, so the staff had to give everyone Ukrainian names.

The hospital was in a school, and the medical staff soon began to engage in underground activities like procuring a receiver so they could listen to the Soviet news, and taking German sacks of corn, along with rifles and even sub-machine-guns. But a German-appointed Russian police officer suspected them, and the hospital was consequently surrounded by German soldiers and local police. They discovered Russians and Jews in the hospital, whereupon the staff and 40 of the wounded were taken away to a prisoner-of-war camp.

Leonid was taken, too. But he even managed to give a speech to local villagers before he went, urging them to struggle against the invaders. Seeing the effect of his speech on the villagers, a German officer cut him short. Ever heroic, as the sleigh took him away, Leonid bit through a vein in his wrist, soaked his handkerchief in blood and threw it out into the crowd declaring, 'See it gets to my sons.'

Leonid was shot on 7 March 1942. A day later,

an escapee handed Leonid's last note to a nurse at the hospital. It was written in pencil on sheets of paper and addressed to his wife and children. When the Soviet forces eventually liberated the area, the nurse managed to get this note to his family.

This is that last, dramatic note which he managed to write just before being executed. The reader cannot help but be impressed by Leonid's passion, ideals and lofty vocabulary.

*My dear wife Anna and boys Lenya and Gennady,*

*I want to hug and kiss you for the last time. Today I am to be shot by order of the German Command.*

*Boys, grow up and get your own back on all fascists for me. As I part from you, I am entrusting you with all my blessed hatred for these vile swine. Cut them down to the last fascist. I've lived honourably, fought honourably and die honourably.*

*I die for our country, for our Party, for all Russians, Ukrainians, Byelorussians and all other people in the country, and for you. Love our country like I love her, fight for her like I have and, if need be, die for her like me.*

*Boys, love and respect and obey your mother, she going to have a hard time bringing you up, but our country and comrades whom I've saved won't leave you in the lurch. Remember every soldier must have one motto: 'I die but don't surrender.' I didn't surrender. I had a concussion, couldn't walk and it wasn't right to desert my badly wounded companions. When we were prisoners, I set up a Soviet colony and saved many lives. I stood by them to the last minute, I've done all I could for my country. Time's running out.*

*My dear ones, be decent Soviet people, grow up to be Bolsheviks. Anna, farewell!! Lenya and Gennady, good-bye!*

*Long live our country!*

*All my love,*

*Your husband and father.*

★    ★    ★

Twenty-eight-year-old Ted Baker was a signalman in the army during World War II. He had a wife, Ruby, and two children, a daughter Pat and a son Peter who grew up to be the famous drummer Ginger Baker.

Ted went missing in action for a year before an

officer discovered marked graves on the Greek island of Leros. He was one of 100 men who were ambushed on the island, 85 of whom were killed. The Germans came in quickly by sea and parachute, and they also outnumbered the British by four to one. The families were told later that the Germans thought they were a special division because they fought so hard. Ted was killed in action on 15 November 1943.

In 1942, Ted had written three last letters – one to his wife, another to his son and a last one to his beloved daughter Pat, who was only four when he died. Her mother, Ruby, gave it to her when she was 14. She says this letter still makes her feel as though her father is watching over her. She says she used to read it when she was upset about something, and it calmed her down. Pat also says this special letter has had an extraordinary effect on her life, that it has made her think about how to live. 'It makes you stop and think about how you treat other people … he instilled that into me. It's as if he's still alive, still there, because of my last letter. I can't remember anything else he ever said to me. That letter filled that void.'

This letter is interesting in what it reveals about values of the era, and touching in his fatherly adoration and how he attempts to look after the relationship between his daughter and his wife in the best possible way.

*My Darling little Pat,*

*I have been thinking things over while waiting for my boat, and as I might not return, I think it is only right that you should have a letter from me which you can keep, to remember me by.*

*I writing this assuming you are now grown up, as you will not receive this till then. I can picture you as a lovely girl, very happy with lots of boyfriends. I am finding it very hard to write this, as I may never see you at this stage. You have always been the pride and joy of my life. I have loved you more than my life and at all times.*

*As mother has told you perhaps, I was always afraid of losing you. Now the tables have turned the other way and I might be the one to get lost. But do not let this upset you if this is the case, as the love for a father only lasts up to the time a girl finds the man she wants and gets married.*

*Well, darling, when this times arises, I hope you*

41

find the right one and he will not only be a good husband to you, but will also make up for the fatherly love you have missed.

At all times, lovie, be a pal to mother and look after her, do what you can to make her happy, as she has been and will always be, I am sure, the best little mother you find on this earth. Don't be selfish or catty, remember there are others in the world as well as you. Try not to talk about people as this gets you disliked. When the pulling to pieces starts, walk out or turn a deaf ear… it will pay in the long run.

Above all, I want you to be a sport, to take up swimming, dancing and all the games in life you can get so much fun out of. Mother, I am sure, will do her best for you and see you get all the instruction she can afford. Always try to be a sister to Peter and John [Pat's cousin], they may pull your leg about different things. But the best way after all is to ignore them and do what you can for them. You will win in the end and be the best of pals.

Well, darling, there is no more I can say, but to look after yourself where men are concerned, be wise and quick witted and only believe half they

*say … of course, till you get the right one.*
*Remember me as your dad and pal who*
*worshipped the ground you walked on. Please*
*don't do anything that will upset mother, and I*
*shouldn't like you to. I will close now, my little ray*
*of sunshine.*

  *Always loving you,*
  *Your Loving,*
  *Father.*
  *xxxxxxxxxxxxxxx*

★　　★　　★

Kamikaze attacks by Japanese pilots were proud
endeavours in which young men like 17-year-old
Yukio Araki were honoured to be asked to die for
their country. Yukio died in a suicide attack on an
American ship near Okinawa on 17 May 1945. He
had left three letters to be opened by his family
when they found out about his death. This one is
remarkable for its simplicity; he is totally
committed to his country and therefore his family.

*Dear Father and Mother*
  *I trust you and my brothers are doing well*
*recently. It has been decided that at last I will go to*

take part in the Battle of Okinawa as a member of a special attack force. I am deeply moved. I only look forward to sinking a ship with a single blow.

When I look back, I apologise for not being devoted to you in any way for some ten years to this day.

Through teaching by various senior officers after I entered the Army, I now devote myself to my country as a special attack force member. Please find pleasure in your desire for my loyalty to the emperor and devotion to parents.

I have no regrets. I just go forward on my path.

I ask that you teach my three younger brothers so they can serve our country as noble airmen. I sincerely hope you take good care of yourselves and make strenuous efforts on the home front.

Please give my regards to all my relatives and to everyone in the neighbourhood association.

Sayonara.

Yukio Araki

72nd Shinbu Squadron

★   ★   ★

Gwyn Williams wrote his last letter to his girlfriend, Betty, the day before he left Malta on

HM Submarine *Usk*. Sadly, she had to read it. Six days later, on 25 April 1941, it hit a mine off Cape Ben and Gwyn and all his comrades were killed.

Generously, Betty gave the letter to his family even though it was hers. It was then left to Gwyn's sister, who has looked after it since 1972 when their parents died. Of course, his grave is the sea, which lends this last letter even more importance for his sister. The official confirmation of his death didn't come until 1945, so they had to wait four years.

In fact, Betty was only 17 when she was going out with Gwyn, and she didn't want to get tied down. He'd wanted to get engaged but she hadn't wanted to rush into a committed relationship.

Gwyn had written this last letter just in case he didn't return from the war. It shows that, despite calling her 'darling', he didn't know her very well but obviously felt passionately for her.

*Dearest Betty,*

*Betty my darling, I think that you won't mind me calling you that for the last time.*

*As I expect by now my sister has informed you that I have died in fighting for our and other countries, but I may say darling that my last thoughts were of my family and you, and I love you while there is a breath in my body.*

*I take this the last opportunity of wishing you the happiest marriage which is possible for two people to have and only wish that it was I. Also give my wishes for a happy and long life to your mother, father and all your friends and relations, and with these few last words I close wishing you all the very best.*

*Your most loving friend,*

*Gwyn*

★   ★   ★

'Zoya' means life in Greek, and this 20-year-old Soviet woman, Zoya Kruglova, was eager to live it to the full. When the war with Germany broke out, she threw herself into useful activities. She helped with putting up defences and evacuating children from Leningrad, taught the local population what to do in air-raids and also took a course in nursing. In the autumn of 1941, she became a medical orderly to the 145th anti-tank battalion. She also started to work for the intelligence on the North-Western Front.

In the winter of 1941, Zoya and two colleagues crossed the front to gather intelligence about German troop movements near Leningrad. Zoya spoke good German and could pass herself off as German. This way, she found out valuable information about the number of German garrisons, landing strips and the movements of their troops which she managed to radio back to HQ. She continued to work gathering intelligence for a couple of years but, in 1943, she and a comrade were seized by the Gestapo. She was sent to a prison for condemned prisoners but managed to escape. But she was eventually recaptured while attempting to cross the front.

Zoya was tortured but her strong spirit never left her. She was bloodied but unbowed. Apparently, she used to sing in defiance and everyone in the prison would listen to her songs. She realised this time there was no escape, but she managed to smuggle a final note out to her family. On 9 September 1943, Zoya was shot by the German troops.

On her cell wall, she managed to write, 'I used to love freedom and the wide-open spaces, that's why it's very hard to get used to being locked up. In Greek, my name, Zoya, means life. Oh, how I want to live, live, live.'

To her family, she wrote this last letter. Zoya is zealous in her commitment to resist the Germans, and she shows huge bravery in this letter, as well as her genuine feelings. She shows she has already accepted that death is inevitable. The reader also understands how important duty is to her.

She also mentions, as many last letters do, that she does not want her family to cry; she can't stand that they will have to grieve for her. It is a very passionate last letter.

*My dear Mum and Dad, dear little sisters Valya, Panya and Shura and dear little brother Borya,*

*I'm writing to you, darlings, from prison for the last time. You will receive this letter when I am dead.*

*My darlings, it's already a year since you received news from me; I've been wandering about all the time but I never forgot about you. They arrested me in February and that makes two-and-a-half months since I've been here alone in a solitary cell. Every day I expected to be taken out and shot.*

*Mummy, things have been pretty grim but I endured it all. They sent me to a camp in Pskov where I stayed two months and escaped back to our side. I was again sent on a mission and again I ended up in this prison – this is the second month. I have been beaten about the head with sticks. Now waiting to be shot. I don't think any more about living though, my dear ones... I very much want to live a bit if only to see you, give you a big hug and cry all my grief away on your breast, Mummy, dear.*

*In fact, if I hadn't landed here a second time, I would have been home in September. But, there it is, it's no use crying over spilt milk. At least, I've done my duty.*

*Mummy, don't take it too badly, don't cry. I would have liked to have consoled you but I'm very far away and behind iron bars and thick walls. I frequently sing songs in gaol, and the whole prison listens.*

*My dear ones, other girls will tell you about me, if they survive... Once more I beg you, don't cry.*

49

*All my love to you all.*

*Farewell forever.*

*My body will be in Ostrov behind the prison by the side of the road. I shall be clothed in my black woollen dress, which is a bit faded now, and the red knitted jumper you bought for me, Mummy, and Russian boots.*

*Your daughter, Zoya*

*Goodbye…*

★   ★   ★

Kenneth Stevens was taken prisoner by the Japanese on 10 February 1942. He and his fellow prisoners had to march to the prisoner-of-war camp in the jungle on the Siam–Burma border and, when they got there, food rations were very low. He spent his days imagining meals at home in all their glorious detail, but at the same time starving. In fact, on 4 April 1943, he wrote his wife, Penelope, a letter which is, in effect, a Will, and he includes all the details of his financial affairs adding, at the end, 'I do hope you marry again and soon, because you are much too marvellous a person to be left alone.' He also writes about what he would like for his son, Christopher, in that he would like him to spend time abroad so he is not narrow-minded and that he would like him to grow up in the country rather than the town.

On 25 May, a hospital was opened up and Kenneth was admitted until 11 June, but there were no medicines and, as a patient, he developed violent diarrhoea, which was the forerunner of cholera. In his diary, he describes himself as skin and bone and weak as a rat.

On 15 June, he wrote his last letter to Penelope, who had been living in Singapore but had recently been reunited with their son, Christopher, at their house in Ilkley, Yorkshire. That last letter gives amazing insights into the terrible conditions there, and what a prisoner-of-war is thinking about during his final days. He also considers their future together and that this experience may well have made him a better human being. Sadly, Penelope was never to find out the effect of his imprisonment upon him. He died on 10 August 1943.

*Penelope my own darling,*

*Life has become extremely grim since I last wrote to you at Changi. I don't want to talk* about it much because I think about you all the time and the sooner I forget the better. But we are in a rather terrible P.O.W camp in the jungle on the Siam–Burma border, 192 miles from Ban Pong in Siam and 80 miles from Madmein in Burma. Food's very scarce and medical supplies also and we are coping with cholera, dysentery and beri-beri – we have lost 160-odd men out of 1,600 in the first 3 weeks but things are slightly better now.

Getting here was rather an ordeal – 3 weeks of marching thro' the jungle at night, everything having to be carried in our packs. It was the most exhausting business and was undoubtedly the cause of so many deaths here as people had very little resistance left. I developed ulcerated sores on my legs and arms about half way thro' the journey but these were really a blessing in disguise as I went into 'hospital' as soon as we arrived here, so I had a good rest. I was in for 18 days and early on got a bit scared as I developed the early signs of cholera so I starved myself completely for 5 days and managed to get over it. It has left me a bag of bones and very weak but I am still lying up so am alright.

I spend the whole time living my life with you

*both in the past and what I hope for in the future. It was an inspiration for you to send that photo of you and Christopher – I looked at it for hours on end, although actually Christopher didn't figure so very much in my thoughts – it was nearly all you – I think it was that I needed so badly.*

*Oh darling, I do so passionately want to come out of this alive to be with you again – I'm sure I'll be such a nicer person and I do want to be able to show you every day of my life how much I appreciate you and all your wonderfulness. I have thought so much of Chancery Hill and what a beautiful home you made of it and how proud I was of it, and of your making a real home out of a Singapore house!*

*In this place, one's mind returns continually and dwells longingly on Food – do you know, darling, that when I think of all the dishes I'd like to be having, it is always in Chancery Hill that I think of eating them because they were always much better there than at anyone else's house or any hotel. I think the only dish I think of elsewhere is Crumbly Cutlets, and I think that is because I don't remember ever having them at home. But when I think of Duck and Cherry Casserole,*

Scrambled Eggs, Fish Scallops, Chicken Stanley, Kedgeree, Trifle, Summer Pudding, Fruit Fool, Bread and Butter Pudding – all those lovely things were made just perfectly 'right' in my own home.

Then there was the time you had coping with the difficulties of Mama and Monty and her baby, all at the same time as you were working endlessly at the hospital. And of course, above all there was our completely wonderful Christopher Michael and I don't think anyone can deny that there were few babies like him in Malaya.

So there you are, darling, as wife, housewife, housekeeper, hostess and mother you were a complete and outstanding success – do you wonder that I feel uncertain as to whether I can ever make up to you for the risks and unhappiness of the last 2 years?

By the way, you have also been wonderful in fixing up the insurance policies for yourself and Christopher's education – you know dearest, that it wasn't slackness on my part that it wasn't done, but due to this nonsense about my old heart but still I'm sorry that you have the trouble of having to do it… I am hoping that the DRC or the Govt are giving you money to live on – there were supposed to have been arrangements made when

54

*we first went out to Changi as POWs but I doubt
if they ever got thro' to England*

*It's getting dark, sweetie, so I must stop. Loving
you so tremendously much all the time.*

*Ken*

★　　★　　★

Lieutenant Sanehisa Uemura, 25, was part of the
Kamikaze Special Attack Corps. He died in battle
in the Philippine Sea area on 26 October 1944.
He was born in Tokyo, and he wrote this sweet,
loving last letter to his young daughter, Motoko,
before he died. The reader is aware of the
harshness of his duty, set against the softness of his
love for his daughter.

*Motoko,*

*You often looked and smiled at my face. You
also slept in my arms, and we took baths together
[a Japanese custom]. When you grow up and
want to know about me, ask your mother and
Aunt Kayo.*

*My photo album has been left for you at home.
I gave you the name Motoko, hoping you would
be a gentle, tender-hearted and caring person.*

*I want to make sure you are happy when you grow up and become a splendid bride, and even though I die without you knowing me, you must never feel sad.*

*When you grow up and want to meet me, please come to Kudan* [Kudan Hill is the location in Tokyo of the Uasukuni Jinja, Japan's national shrine to honour the spirits of soldiers killed in battle]. *And if you pray deeply, surely your father's face will show itself within your heart. I believe you are happy. Since your birth you started to show a close resemblance to me, and other people would often say that when they saw little Motoko, they felt like they were meeting me. Your uncle and aunt will take good care of you with you being their only hope, and your mother will only survive by keeping in mind your happiness throughout your entire lifetime. Even though something happens to me, you must certainly not think of yourself as a child without a father. I am always protecting you. Please be a person who takes loving care of others.*

*When you grow up and begin to think about me, please read this letter.*

*Father*

*P.S. In my airplane, I keep as a charm a doll you had as a toy when you were born. So it means Motoko was together with Father. I tell you this because my being here without your knowing makes my heart ache.*

\*　　\*　　\*

Twenty-one-year-old Eric Rawlings was the wireless operator and air gunner on Wellington R1463 based at Snaith in Yorkshire. Returning from a raid on the night of 21 February 1942, the aircraft flew into a hill in Asterby, Lincolnshire. Eric and three others were killed.

From Muswell Hill in London, his father Frank said of him after his death, 'He perfectly fulfilled all we ever hoped of him.' Aware that his actions with the RAF were fraught with danger in operations over Germany, Eric went ahead and wrote a last letter just in case he didn't return, and gave it to his brother, Norman, for safekeeping. Eric finds wonderful ways of expressing his love for his family. He also makes it very clear that he is fighting in this war to protect the future of his kinsmen and that it is an ideological sacrifice.

*Dearest Folks,*

*Now that I'm on operational work and admitting that the risk is fairly considerable, I thought I would just put a few words on paper which you could keep as a remembrance in case anything should happen to me.*

*In the revoltingly chaotic world today where everyone is fighting and killing everyone else, it has always been wonderful just to take my thoughts from worldly beastliness and to think of the things which I revere and esteem most in the world – my family and my home.*

*Love is such a very difficult thing to express here and now on paper, but I only hope that I've made you all understand and realise the depth of my love and the gratitude for everything which you have done for me.*

*Whenever there's fighting going on anywhere, you can always hear the words from people not involved – 'Half of them don't know what they're fighting about anyway.' Which is usually true. Well, I know what I'm fighting for. I'm fighting so that in the future people will have the chance to live as happily as we all did together before the War without interference. Where young un's like myself could make the most of the marvellous opportunities which you gave me for 20 years and for which I know you made many sacrifices. God bless you all, and may everything turn out right in the end.*

*God bless you again,*
*Your adoring son and 'Little One'*

★   ★   ★

Senior Lieutenant Yevgeny Chervonny served on a torpedo boat in the Baltic fleet. In July 1942, he put to sea in an operation which he knew he had practically no chance of surviving. His body was picked up after the boat hit a mine.

Yevgeny was totally opposed to fascism. He'd already experienced Franco's men during the Spanish Civil War who had tried to make the Soviet seaman betray their country when they'd captured his ship. The Soviets ended up in prison and the young Yevgeny arrived home sick because he'd contracted TB. Once he was cured, his attitude to fascism was already ingrained within him. When the war came, he was determined that Nazism would not survive, and he swore to fight to his last drop of blood and win.

Fiercely determined, Yevgeny shot down two planes personally from their torpedo boat and was awarded the Order of the Red Banner.

His last letter to his wife was found in a yellow case among his belongings. It is a brilliant combination of high-flown language, philosophy, courage, commitment, love and memories. He was obviously a great character and hero.

*Darling Talyushka*

*It's hard to begin with common words. When you receive this letter, I shall no longer be alive. But there we are, we have to take what comes in life.*

*Life! The word has such a proud ring. It contains grief and good cheer, suffering and bliss. I'm not going to say life's all the same to me. Not at all, it means a lot. And it's darn hard to lose it.*

*Youth! What can be dearer than that? I'm not one of the 'Dismal Desmonds bearing death with a tirade of curses'. No one should play with life. Not to say we shouldn't be afraid of danger. The boys on shore don't have to run so many risks. But I, like so many of my companions, plumped for the sea where there's a greater element of danger and risk. Here a person can really extend himself to the full and do most good. More simply, it was an urge to throw in all I have.*

*Life can be just a round of daily vegetation like a dumb animal, and life can be free and easy, with wonderful things to look forward to. All of us strive to sling our hammock onto the latter. Our generation has been entrusted with a great and responsible task: to shed our blood and lay down our lives to earn the right to happiness.*

*I remember when I was a lad at school. My first timid steps when I took my school certificate. The first test – 1938–39 – in a prison camp in Spain. That's where I was jolted out of part of the benevolence and habit of seeing everything in a rosy hue, which every young lad and lass does. It was a good lesson in the attempt to understand life. There in Spain I got a fair idea of what we were up against. As a result, I decided to devote my whole life to the armed forces, to become an officer. Now you are getting a taste of hatred. It came to me in those days.*

*Calm and peaceful 1940. A year of stupendous plans for the future. Then came the war. Everyone was faced with the problem of finding his feet and being a worthy son of his country. The old feeling* of hatred, the invasion of my beloved Ukraine, losing my father, mother and brother, the realisation that the fight was universal and there was no relying on anyone, aided me right from those early days to decide where I stood and what I was going to do. War came as a test, it put the finishing touches to my character. I gave it all I had. And I can honestly say that nobody can reproach me for any action unworthy of an officer and a Communist.

We were forced to see life in the raw, cruelly and in a much shorter time than age usually allows, but life will be all the dearer to us. Once you know how dear life really is you don't treat it so lightly as the days go by. I know and am confident that if I'd have got out of this mess in one piece we'd have been so happy together... We live in a time when before we can lay claim to that happiness, we have to win it in stubborn combat and do our own little bit for the common cause. It makes no difference whether it will be the skill, blood or life. There is no other way.

Remember me now and again as the man who loved you and would lay down his life for his Talyushka without a thought. And that's how it really is. In every common cause there's a part of every man. And for what I gave my part is your cause too. I believed in your love knowing it was crystal clear. It's so wonderful to think of all the times we've been together...

I know it won't be easy for you to get over the idea of losing your Zhenya. But please, dear, don't make any foolish pledges. Try to bury all the grief quickly. Try and make your life happy. I'd like to think that in a little while you will forget it all or at least get over it and be happy again. To every man his own fate. There's no getting away from it.

I'd like to say a word of gratitude to your mother, father and little Zoya. They really have looked on me as a son. I wish them a long and happy carefree life. I hope your parents and Zoya will one day have some grandchildren, sons and nieces to nurse and make a fuss of.

One request to you. Once the war is over and life gets back to normal, try and find my young brother if you can. If he's alive, the country will look after him. He should be a big lad now. Tell him about his Zhenya. Put him on the right lines. His name is Alexander, born in 1930 and left behind in Kherson. I comfort myself that *you'll find him. Don't think this is some kind of last wish or an order to look after him. I don't want to burden you with a load of trouble. In our country, they look after children and make men out of them. I'm sending you the certificate of my award. Let it be a little souvenir. I don't have anything else.*

*That's about all. There's so much I want to say, I want to find some tender words to express my feelings. But you know your Zhenya well enough and you understand, don't you, without me writing it down.*

*Keep your pecker up, look after yourself and put your best foot forward. Be a clever little girl. Don't take it too much to heart. It doesn't help much, you know. Try to make a happy life for yourself and live it for both of us.*

*Remember your Zhenya now and again, but without any tears and with the thought that he didn't die in vain.*

*Keep your spirits up.*

*I love you,*

*Yevgeny*

Twenty-seven-year-old Lieutenant Yonetsu Yoshitaro wrote a last letter to his stepmother and brother before setting off on a mission with the Kamikaze Special Attack Group Fugoku. He was killed near Luzon Island on 13 November 1944. These last letters from kamikaze pilots were significantly different in that the writers knew with certainty that they were going to die. There was no doubt in their minds that their deaths were a sacrifice for their country.

Consequently, their letters are more about honour and ideals than genuine emotions. They cannot afford really to feel what they are about to do, or else doubt may enter into the equation. This last letter is typically noble but impenetrable on a personal level.

*Honorable Older Brother,*

*Once again, orders have come down for the attack from which we will never return. I feel not the slightest regret. Already I have grown intimate with death, the ultimate character-building passage that we human beings have to face. All that is left is to carry out the duties for which I've* been trained and to fulfil the Imperial mandate. I am deeply ashamed that in the 27 years of my life I have been such an unworthy son and younger brother. I will have to leave everything up to you. It is with an untroubled heart that I fulfil the obligations for which I was born.

I am merely carrying out my duties as a man. The Manila bar of toilet soap you'll find in my things was given to me by the Chief of Staff. Please take good care of mother and take care of yourself in the coming winter.

Honorable Mother, forgive the impiety of my premature departure.

Yonetsu Yoshitaro

# 3
## World War I

The World War I last letters are even more formal; their writing is often full of flowery expressions, and the first two show a deliberate avoidance of expressing loving feelings in a direct manner. This is stiff-upper-lip country, but that doesn't mean these soldiers didn't have just the same feelings underneath. Once again, their wish to thank their families and save them suffering is very much in evidence. They also explore what death means to them in different ways.

★　　★　　★

Twenty-four-year-old Second Lieutenant Norman Herbert Smith had been a scholarship boy at Bradford Grammar School in West Yorkshire and was an only child. At the time that he was called up, Norman had been offered a place at Oxford University to read Classics and planned to take up this place when he left the army.

Norman was killed on the first day of the battle of Cambrai in France during 1917 by a sniper while he was leading his platoon at Havrincourt.

Norman wrote this last letter to his parents

*Norman Herbert Smith*

shortly before his death, and it was printed in the local *Bradford Observer* as an example of a beautifully written last letter.

The paper wrote in December 1917, 'As though to prepare his parents for the worst news they could receive in respect of himself and to mitigate the great grief which his death would bring them, he closed the letter with words so deeply affecting in the light of what has happened, and yet so comforting to his parents as showing the spirit of calm and high courage with which he faced the fate which he realised might be his.'

This is a classic example of a formal type of World War 1 last letter; Norman's preoccupations are saving his parents from worrying, and reconfirming the justice and ideals of his role as a soldier. It is lofty in its tones but nevertheless it illustrates his devotion to his mother and father, and his country.

*Dear Mother and Father*

*We must not shrink from the facts, however disquieting they may appear. Therefore my object is to affirm that neither have I any cause to worry,* nor – and more especially – have you any cause to trouble on my behalf.

First, from the broadest outlook, we all agree that we are fighting for ideals, which will improve the world, and the lives of generations to come, so we are fighting with high religious motives. Again, we are fighting for our country, which is among all the nations the noblest work one can perform.

There is, moreover, the personal element, for in this struggle, I am your representative. You have given to me all that I could have wished for, and more than I could have expected, among many things a sound education, the value of which I realise more and more, and owing to which I was enabled to take my present position. For this I cannot hope to repay you sufficiently, but in some measure I am trying to do so by representing you here.

Finally, it is assured that all who lay down their lives shall reap a rich reward, and shall be like Wordsworth's Happy Warrior, who 'While the mortal mist is gathering draws his breath in confidence of heaven's applause'. Therefore, I repeat that none of us have cause for worry, and I hope you will accept this letter in the spirit in which it is written. This letter is, of course, serious

*in tone but I myself am as fit as ever I was, and*
*am in the best of spirits.*

*Your loving son,*
*Norman*

★　　★　　★

Lieutenant Norman Chamberlain was in the 1st
Battalion of the Grenadier Guards, and was killed
on the Western Front in October 1917. At first,
his family didn't know what had happened to
him but, finally, a Captain who had been fighting
at Norman's side gave an exact description to
Norman's sister of the events, but he had no idea
where he was.

Enid, Norman's sister, writes to one of his
friends, 'the order was given to our people to
retire, which they did into a trench… apparently,
my brother never got the order, and went on
further… no one seems to know how far he got
exactly.' Afterwards, he and seven others had
disappeared, despite search parties being sent out.

At first, the family wanted to believe he was
missing but may be found; for instance, that he
could have been taken prisoner. His sister writes,
'I only hope this suspense won't last much

longer.' But, by February 1918, his family had received a letter saying Norman's body had been found in no man's land and around him were 18 Grenadiers and 20 Germans. According to Enid's letter, the British soldiers 'had caught the Germans in the open with the bayonet, and then the Germans had fired a machine-gun at them, so it was a fight to the death.' She writes proudly, 'Certain it is that a man cannot die a finer death— in the very forefront of battle, for his country. It is a wonderful memory we have of him, but at this time one loses sight of this in part, in the overwhelming sense of loss.'

Norman wrote a last letter to his close group of friends in the army, and asked Enid to send it to them if he died. This last letter demonstrates just how important comradeship was during this war, and those old-fashioned qualities of endurance, friendship, helping each other out and stoicism.

*1st Grenadier Guards*
*My dear boys,*
*  You won't get this unless I'm knocked out, and I'm writing it, not because I think I will, but*

because, if I did go under, I should hate to feel I'd gone without saying goodbye to you all, and wishing you as happy a life and one as worth living as mine. We've been a very happy family — and all our rows and failures and disappointments have only made it all the more worthwhile, because we've generally speaking been able to put things right and learn from experience — both you and I.

I don't know anything, except my love for my mother and sisters, which has made life so pleasant to me as your friendship and companionship; seeing all the pluck and cheerfulness, and unselfishness and real up-hill struggling to keep your end up and make headway — which I've seen in all of you one time or another.

And don't forget that nothing worth doing is done without failures for the time being, without misunderstandings and without a damned lot of unpleasantness.

We've all been able to help one another a lot — go on doing that amongst the Club and amongst your own families.

And I think somehow you'll feel that I can still sympathise with your bad luck and all the unfairness and difficulties that surround one when *one is trying to make good – even if I'm not there to tell you so, and keep you at it.*

*Anyway, keep on pegging away, don't be downhearted and don't forget.*

*Your old pal,*

Norman Chamberlain

★   ★   ★

Captain EF Lubbock was a pilot in World War I. His mother, Lady Avebury, who was based in London, saved his letters. Eric was an observer flying with Major Robert Lorraine when they shot down a German Albatross warplane in October 1915. They were both awarded military crosses for this, and his mother refers to their success as a 'plucky effort'.

He wrote his last letter to his mother in November 1915 with strict instructions that it only be sent to her if he was killed. Sadly, it did have to be posted. He was shot down by Germans whilst on a mission to photograph the line patrols on 11 March 1917. In this letter, he muses on the meaning of life and death, as well as very clearly expressing his love for his family. So it is personal, idealistic and philosophically probing.

*Captain EF Lubbock*

*My darling Mum,*

*One is here confronted almost daily with the possibility of Death, and when one looks forward to the next few months this possibility becomes really a probability. I am therefore settling down now to write to you briefly a few words which, in the event of my death, I hope may help to comfort and to cheer you. Also I know that if in my last hour, I am conscious, my chief consolation will be to feel that these thoughts may reach you. I shall therefore simply write down my ideas about it all and I hope thereby to enable you to feel that though I may be taken away yet that fact is not all grief.*

*Now one of the questions one asks oneself about it all is do you fear Death? And I have I think convinced myself that I do not. My reasons for this I will show later. Of course it is the natural instinct of a human being to avoid Death in all possible ways, 'Life every man holds dear', yes, and every animal of God's holds this great gift dear, but whereas an animal holds life dear only by instinct, it is I think our especial privilege to hold life dear for reasons.*

*Now my reasons are two 1) love and ambition*

2) that I know my death would cause pain to you and I don't want to do that. My love is firstly love for you, secondly love for others, and thirdly love for the world in general. I love you and all my brothers and sisters and friends, and as you know I have loved one person very, very deeply for several years, but of that I will speak later. My love for you and for my brothers and sisters and friends makes me long for life because with it I hope to be able to help you all and add to your happiness. And my love for Dad makes me want to live because I hope that perhaps in some small way I might carry on one of his great works and in so doing honour him. My love for the world in general makes me hope that before I go I may be able to make it in some way (however small) just a bit better than I found it.

Ambition I should perhaps better call interest, it is simply the desire to learn something more of this wonderful and beautiful world before I leave it.

And the other reason, which is more the cause of my dreading death than anything, is why I am writing now.

To fear or dread death for its own sake is

absolutely against all reason, and I want to point out to you that you must not grieve too much if I die.

You, my poor Mummy, suffer a lot from sleeplessness. But suppose now that you went off to sleep at 10 one night and woke up at 8 next morning having had no dream or consciousness at all… would not that seem to you a blessed 10 hours? Now death at its very worst is that, absolute blank, and therefore why fear it?

But I do not believe that death is that. I believe that it is something very different.

You and I know very well that there is what we call right and wrong. We also know that if there is right there must be reward for right doing, and if there is wrong there must be punishment. Now in this world that is not always so, for many are happier and 'better off' as we call it for doing wrong. Now if this world were the end then our wonderful consciousness, and our knowledge of right and wrong is 'altogether vanity', and life is a hopeless failure. If this world is the final end, this imperfect world with all its sorrows and griefs, if this is the best we can attain to then the Great Giver of Life is but a torturer and if you love me you will rejoice that I have left so miserable an existence and lost so painful a consciousness before I suffer any more.

But the very fact that we do know and believe in doing right, in kindness and in love, the very fact of love itself, seems to prove that this world is not the end. It proves to my mind that there is a Something which gave us knowledge and power and which will bring us to the full understanding of purity of love and of God.

Then we can feel that 'Death is a path that must be trod, If man would ever pass to God'.

If then I leave this world to enter a fuller, better and happier world need you grieve for me that I'd so? Oh let your love conquer pain and bless the chance that brings me to eternal joy.

What I have meant to say is that either Death is the end or not the end. That it should be the end is inconceivable, and if it is not the end then that which comes after must be better and higher than this world.

I do not attempt to imagine what is after Death.

There are many, many things, which buffet one when one thinks of them but this seems to me to be the most impossible of all problems to solve. Just as a child has no idea of what life is really like, so can we have no idea of after-life. But I do believe that this world is our nursery and that we are being trained to make us fit for another and better life.

Of course, I know that this is not going to relieve you of the first pangs of parting. You will say I might have been spared for some time to help and comfort you. Yes and I hope I may be spared. We mortals have such deep feelings in the world that it is inevitable that we should have pain at parting. But I hope that you will let me help you even if I am not alive, by believing as I do that we cannot judge for ourselves, and that we cannot here on earth see everything in true proportion. Is not the sorrow of a child when it loses its doll a very real and great grief? And yet, although it is not much use saying to the child, we know that it doesn't much matter.

So Mummy, if you love me, try not to let it be too great a blow to you, try and conquer your own sorrow and to live cheerfully. You have great work before you in caring for Moke and in bringing him up to be the great and good man he is going to be. And you have got to help Urtie, who, although she is so wonderfully strong and good, needs help *to bring up her children, and help which you more than anyone can give. Live for them cheerfully.*

*And in conclusion, I give my very best love to them all — Moke, Urtie, Weenie, Haddie (God protect him) and all the children and to dear Johnnie, to whom I feel grateful and indeed we all must do. He has shown great love and great kindness to us all. And give my love to Bessie and to my friends.*

*And to one friend particularly, Winifred, whom I have always loved. I tried hard not to love her, and even though I found I couldn't help it, for some time I did not admit it to myself. Now I do, and I know what it is to love. God bless her and keep her always happy.*

*So with all my love my darling Mum I now say goodbye, just in case. Try to forget my faults and to remember me only as your loving little son.*

*Eric Lubbock*

*This was written some time ago. Now I have again suffered the most awful pain a man can suffer, that of losing the girl he loves. I know that in your heart you fear that it may make me reckless. It will not, you must trust me that I have strength enough not to let it. But, Mummy, could you see her for my sake and tell her that to the end I loved her. Be kind to her.*

[Evidently, Norman's mother did not approve of Winifred!]

⋆　⋆　⋆

Private David Martin, a 28-year-old from Belfast, was one of a small group of soldiers who were left behind during the British retreat in 1914; as a result, they were trapped behind the lines in German-occupied France.

For 18 months, David and three other British soldiers were hidden by French farmers in a little village near the Somme. But they were eventually betrayed, tried as spies and shot by a German firing squad.

A cook in his civilian life, David enlisted in the Royal Irish Fusiliers and was sent to France in August 1914, leaving his wife and baby daughter in Belfast.

On a typewriter provided by his German captor, David wrote to his wife Mary. He wasn't educated and his last letter is badly spelled and full of grammatical mistakes, but nevertheless it is extremely moving to read. Ninety years later, this extraordinary letter was found in an attic in Hastings.

His poor wife never received his letter but it was found in the personal possessions of a World War I veteran who died in 1977. No one knows how he got hold of it.

*Dear Mary*

*Germans shot me for nothing. I never surrender – the true words of a British soldier. We die happy knowing our (side) is winning. We will win the war for you my dear wife and child... I go to die now. I am not afraid to die.*

*Your loving husband,*

*David*

★   ★   ★

Second Lieutenant GC Jackson was serving as a junior officer and wrote this last letter to his mother shortly before his death on the first day of the Battle of Loos. It is dated 23 September 1915. In it, he expresses his deep religious conviction and the comfort he derived from the prayer book, which his mother gave him.

This seems to be three letters but, in fact, is only one. It becomes a last letter where he is considering his own mortality in the second part. The reader understands what a role his faith has upon his wellbeing, and how devoted he is to his mother.

*My own darling Mamma,*

*I got your letter and it has completely cheered me up. I am afraid one rather lets oneself grouse and grumble when things don't go quite as one wants them.*

*We are having lovely weather, but it gets cold at nights and winter is already beginning.*

*I got Daddy's letter and enclosures. I had a letter from Darby last night and I was very pleased to get it as I hadn't heard from him for a long time. I do hope Edith will have the best of luck and that everything will go off very successfully.*

*Well, I hope with luck to get some leave soon but I don't know when. If Arthur Vershoyle is now home, I am the only one of the family out here.*

*The fruit arrived safely but the bananas did not travel too well, they might be even greener still; the fish is another great treat which we all appreciate.*

*Well darling Mamma, I don't think I have any more news and hoping to see you all again soon. With very best love to you all, I remain ever*

*Your loving*

*Conway*

*I hope Daddy is keeping better.*

*(For you only)*

*I was looking at the text for the 26th evening in DL [his prayer book] and thoroughly believe in it and it has given me new strength and I am taking no thoughts for the morrow but trusting explicitly in Christ and I know he won't forsake me, but will be beside me all through. If anything happens, you will know I was ready for it, and went cheerfully and thankfully to meet my God.*

*How many things I have to thank you and Daddy for. I know I have always been an anxiety to you both as I am afraid I am very headstrong and have always thought of myself first.*

*For Mamma*

*Mamma once asked me what it felt like being under fire; one hasn't much time for one's thoughts at the time, but when it is over I think one's first* thoughts are to thank God for keeping one safe.

When going into the trenches for the first time, I was so interested in everything, and I hardly realised that we were going into the real thing… one thing I notice is that the men always keep watching their officer's every action and if they see you cheery and doing just as you would do under ordinary circumstances it bucks them up enormously. I must say so far I have always been perfectly happy and confident that whatever happens to me will be all for the best, even when going over at night in front of our trenches either to shoot off rifle grenades or for purposes of recognisance, although it is nervy work. I have always felt I was not alone but that God's presence was very near me and I felt just the same when I was opened fire upon on two occasions, and the bullets were whizzing all over my head. You have no idea how it comforts me to know and feel that He is near and looking after me.

Well darling Mama, I think this is all I can tell you… I wish I could tell you in person, as it is so much easier than writing.

With very much love to you all,
Your loving Conway

# 4
## Incidental Wartime Farewells

Naturally, writing a last letter deliberately before death causes the writer to examine his or her life, thoughts and feelings at that moment; an incidental last letter, however – one which becomes a last letter by pure chance – is a completely different type of writing. Often light-hearted and full of the minutiae of everyday wartime existence, they inform the reader about the mundane in a colourful way, whether they are contemporary letters or older ones.

The contemporary ones illustrate both the horrific danger and the soldier's innocence going hand in hand. As for letters from previous wars, I found it strangely compelling to read about pilot Sergeant Eric Skinner's enjoyment of his bombing outings in World War II and began to appreciate what pleasure such danger created. I was also able to understand how World War I soldiers relished the arrival of their parcels from home and how such small luxuries like oranges meant so much in a wartime situation.

★　　★　　★

Nineteen-year-old Kingsman, Jamie Hancock, from Lancashire, had been in Iraq for two weeks when he started his first ever sentry duty at the Old State Building in Basra. Within moments, he was killed by a bullet that was later discovered to be British. It was the type of bullet used in SA80 rifles that were being used by British soldiers on duty that day. The MOD is investigating whether Jamie was killed by friendly fire. Body armour on his back didn't protect him in this case, with the bullet passing through his shoulder and chest, in all likelihood, killing him instantly. The other possibility is that Iraqi insurgents had managed to get hold of one of these rifles during the fighting.

His father, Eddie, 60, of Hindley Green, Lancashire, said at the time, 'It makes no difference to Jamie whether he was killed accidentally by one of his own side or by insurgents. He still died a hero and a man, serving his Queen and his country. I get some comfort from the thought that he would have died instantly without suffering.'

Jamie had written a letter to his father the night before, and it was winging its way to the UK as his body arrived at RAF Brize Norton. His father went to meet his son's coffin which was draped in the Union flag, despite this not being protocol.

'I had to go to him,' he said at the time. 'It's not protocol, they don't like it, but I had to. You want to open up the casket and cradle him, but you can't. I just kissed it. I said, "Welcome home, soldier. Your family and your nation are proud of you."'

His company commander, Major Chris Job, described him as an 'energetic and enthusiastic individual who lived for the army and had a very promising career ahead of him. His enthusiasm was boundless and the fearless spirit with which he lived was amply demonstrated by his decision to volunteer for this Iraq tour.'

His father also let it be known that this was a war which he thought soldiers should not have been asked to fight in.

Jamie's funeral took place at the local church where he was christened. His coffin was carried by nine members of his battalion to the accompaniment of 'The Lark Ascending' by Vaughan Williams. A montage of photos of Jamie as a child, a teenager and a soldier were passed around and, outside, crowds listened to the service, which was broadcast to them. Jamie's mother, Lynda – who is divorced from his father – had written an open letter to her precious son, which was read out. She had written, 'You were so full of life, we will remember you and your favourite things – Scott, your best friend, nights out with the boys… and the girls, of course… at Barbarella's, Wigan Pier music, "proper" food at McDonald's, and Kentucky Family Buckets just for you.' She signed this tender letter, 'Sleep tight, J. Love always, Mum xxx.'

Jamie's 24-year-old brother, Joe, was also a soldier, and was stationed at the barracks in North Yorkshire where Jamie was stationed before going to Iraq. An army chaplain read out a statement from him, which said, 'To be a soldier is in our blood. It's not something that can be given, only earned,' he said. 'We give our lives to be the best, and leave our family, friends and home to fight for what we believe to be right. We train and fight in conditions that shock people, and we do it because we love what we do. Jamie died a man, a hero and, most of all, for Queen and country. How many young men have that sort of commitment today?'

Jamie hadn't intended his final written words to be a last message to loved ones; in fact, he obviously was far from thinking about his own death. Ironically, despite almost being hit by a rocket, this last letter is full of youthful enthusiasm for his work and about how much he likes Basra. Also his use of expressions like 'Fuck me' and 'I shit myself' sit in such stark contrast to the euphemistic letters of previous wartime periods. It is shockingly unknowing. It's almost as though he views his time in Basra with the eyes of a tourist – 'This place is amazing, Dad, it's all made of marble. I have taken a few pictures of it…' – as well as a soldier. He seems mentally so distant from his own mortality. This makes his death seem all the more tragic.

*Hi Dad,*

*I am now in Basra Palace. I am going to the Old State Building tomorrow. It's really mad here. I got here last night.*

*The weather is getting cooler. It rains about now to December. I had my first rocket attack about two hours ago. I was on the roof just looking at the view and I heard a whizzing noise and then*

95

*a big bang. Fuck me. I shit myself. One of the rockets didn't explode, it went straight through the toilets. Unlucky. ☺*

*Basra looks really nice. This place is amazing Dad, it's all made of marble. I have taken a few pictures of it. I will show you when I get home. Thanks for all the foot creams and powders, they came in handy.*

*Okay, love you loads, tell Joe [his brother], I love him too.*

*Jamie*

★   ★   ★

George Cope (also known as Arthur) from Chadwell Heath, Essex, was a wireless operator, flying out of Millennial during the latter part of World War II. He was killed on take-off on 22 March 1945 on his third operation. His wife always thought he'd been killed over the sea but the family now realise, through research, that he died at Munford Cover in Thetford.

This last letter to his parents was written the day before the crash. He certainly didn't mean it to be his final farewell. The most interesting part concerns his second operation at Hamm and how it is 'one mass of bomb craters', and how they could see from the plane 'the trail of a V2 which had just been fired off in Germany on its way to London'. The rest is mundane detail about his daily life and worries. But the sad truth is that he was killed the next day.

*Dear Mum and Dad*

*Thanks so much for your letter received on Monday and I was pleased to see you were OK and Dad is still improving. I am still well myself.*

*Yesterday I did my second operation on the large railway marshalling yards at Hamm, east of Ruhr. There was the usual amount of flak which was accurate, one or two bursts too close to be comfortable. There wasn't much cloud so we could see the target. Below me Hamm is one mass of bomb craters, we could see them well even at the height we were.*

*After we had left the target we saw the trail of a V2 which had just been fired off in Germany on its way to London I suppose. It came right under the plane.*

*I was pleased to hear John is home at last and I was hoping to see him. You see we should get leave starting on April 10th but we have been put* down for April 17th. Well, I told Johnnie that John was home and asked him to try to get our leave at the proper time but he just said he wasn't interested so I guess I shan't see John after all unless they put it forward themselves.

I haven't done anything at nights since I wrote on Sunday, I haven't been off the camp at all. Went to the pictures on Monday night to see 'Three Men in White' which was quite good. I have been feeling quite fed up with Johnnie's attitude since he told us our leave wasn't until the 17th. You can bet your bottom dollar that if and when I have to do a second tour after this one I shan't get an Australian skipper.

The weather around here is keeping quite nice too except for one or two days when it turned a bit chilly.

Yes, I have been hearing quite a bit from Tom lately but it might be quite a time before I hear again as there has been a big gap in my letters to him. I also remembered you to Alf when I wrote.

Well, I will close again for now. Please remember me to John. Take care of yourselves.

Your loving son

Arthur

★   ★   ★

Sergeant Eric Skinner was part of an RAF bomber crew during World War II. He was stationed at Upper Leyland in Oxfordshire between May and July 1940. During this period, he wrote 18 letters to his girlfriend, Jean. He was flying Hampden bombers on night raids over Germany, but was reported missing on 30–31 August 1940. The carefully tended graves of the crew were found at the end of the war in a Catholic churchyard in Holland. Later, they were transferred to a British cemetery.

His mother wrote to Jean on 9 September 1940 thanking her for her flowers and kind thoughts. During this period, they didn't know for sure that Eric was dead so she writes, 'We are all very sad but still hopeful that our dear Eric is still alive and well, he has an even chance.' At that time, she was still hoping to hear from him soon and says, 'Bless him, he was so full of hope and what he was going to do for England, he was so proud of the RAF.' She also adds that his Captain had written to say 'he was a splendid, gallant human who will be greatly missed by them all'. Their vicar had written a prayer and she says she was finding it a great help and ends by asking Jean to keep hoping and praying with them.

Eric wrote this last letter to Jean shortly before he went missing in action. He's obviously not thinking about his eventual demise, although he does mention his luck holding, but is more intent on showing her what an exciting time he's having, especially during the bombing raids. Notably, he writes about 'the lovely twists and turns' their plane makes just after a duel with a German plane, which graphically illustrates the thrill of war. It's obvious from his last letter how much Eric loves being in the RAF and the pleasure that he derives from flying, often even more on dangerous missions.

*My dear Jean*

*Since my return, I have been very busy… one [of] our kites lobbed down in the sea after a raid on Wednesday night. At 11.00 Thursday morning I went out on a sweep (search would be a better word), the sweep lasted 6 hours, we came back to base having met with no success. Other planes went out on Thursday and Friday, the last one back on the latter day sighted the crew in a rubber boat. The wireless operator got a bearing and came* back, we thought it was all over. This soon proved not to be so — at 2.30am Sat: I was dragged out of bed and was on a dawn patrol 2 hours later, we searched for 6 and a half hours and failed to find any trace, after our return more crews went but all came back with thumbs down. I went to bed at 2.00pm and slept until 8.00, when I had supper and went to bed after an hour in the mess.

If things had gone to plan I would now be flying my way through a hoard of Mess 109s. We were in the plane all set to take off when our raid was cancelled, I really was annoyed. I suppose I should be pleased in a way. The job we were going on was very dangerous, only half the planes were expected back. I'm sorry I cannot tell you what the target was, it would have been a great flight, that's all I can say.

Isn't the weather glorious, just right for holidays, it's a pity so many people have been forced to give them up. Perhaps this time next year, things will be getting back to normal. Even if the war is over, I'll still be in the RAF, that's if my luck still holds of course.

The pilot I was going with tonight is an Australian, he wears an Oxford Blue uniform with gold braid — quite smart, he also has the

DFC. This would have been his first raid in seven weeks. On his last trip he had a lump of shrapnel in the shoulder, the observer was killed, wireless op. hit 12 times and gunner – not a scratch! This proves I think that the gunner always gets the worst of the battle. Another of our pilots has won the DFC… he has not had the presentation yet, he celebrated his 21st birthday yesterday. Will close down for the night now. Goodnight Jean. Will finish off tomorrow. I hope I am not suffering from that Monday morning feeling.

Well nothing happened during the day, at 8.30pm we took off for Germany, it was rather a long trip. We met intense AA fire, it was very exciting. Things went as usual until we had just dropped our bombs, then the great thing happened.

We were attacked by two fighters. One came in to 100 yards, we had a duel and to great relief, the Nazi broke off the engagement. After the fight we ran into more gunfire, we did some lovely twists and turns in evasive action. I got to bed at 5.00am, slept until around 3.00pm. I am just off to Doncaster to the flicks.

Cheerio – write soon

Love Eric

★   ★   ★

Herbert Coolum was on a troop ship, *SS Yoma*, which crossed the path of a German U-boat on 17 June 1943 and sank. He was reported missing and, in February 1944, the Army Council informed the family that it was presumed that he had been killed in action.

During the war, he was befriended in Algeria by a young girl called Viviane who welcomed him into her family home and wrote about him. 'Bert was our big English brother whom we loved very much. He often stayed with us. We always waited impatiently for his days leave, and when he arrived with his great friend, George, the house was full of life and happiness. Alas one day, he told us about his pending departure. All of us, the little ones too, cried, we were so attached to him.'

In his last letter home, he asked about his auntie's wedding which he had missed. He was engaged to be married to a woman called Margaret.

*Dear Mum*

*Well, Mum, how did the wedding go? I was thinking of you all on Saturday travelling in a*

*cattle truck and I was wishing I was with you. I
hope that you and Emie got my airgraph all right.
I only wish I had the same chance to get married
but I guess my poor Margaret will have to wait
many long months yet …*

\*    \*    \*

Frederick Charles Hanley, 21 years old, from
Leicester, was an apprentice sheet metalworker
and member of the Home Guard at the
beginning of World War II. He was on fire-
watching duty at a local engineering works
when, fatefully, he chose to make up a bed which
was near the gas stove; unfortunately, other fire-
watchers had left the gas on by mistake. They had
been boiling water to make tea but, instead, the
gas poured into the mess room where the two
young volunteers were sleeping.

Fred died of gas poisoning in the night. His
death was written about in the *Leicester Mercury*
on 30 September 1999 as part of their historical
reports entitled 'The Day the War Broke Out'.
'Death was in the spin of a coin when two young
Second World War Leicester fire-watchers on
duty for the very first time tossed a coin for

*Frederick Charles Hanley*

which of them should have the camp bed. The loser – Frederick Charles Hanley (21) of Cambridge St, Leicester – elected to make up a bed on a table which was near a gas stove.' Both men suffered from coal gas poisoning but the other man, William Siddell (22), recovered.

Fred's brother, who kept his last letter, says, 'My brother, like the millions of others who lost their lives in the Second World War, died in the service of his country. He will never be forgotten as a great, loving and thoughtful big brother.'

Fred wrote a last letter to his father who was serving in the Royal Navy on the *HMS Drake* at Devonport in 1940. He uses this opportunity to describe his appreciation of his parents and his aims for the future, at the time of his coming of age, his 21st birthday. It is interesting to see how his father influenced him to avoid drinking alcohol, and how much he respects his father for making a good home for his family, and sending money home as opposed to spending it on drink. Fred was evidently profoundly influenced morally by his father and, touchingly, found a way to express his gratitude before he died. Poignantly, it is his first and last letter to his father. Sadly, he never reached 22. Fred died on 12 January 1941.

*Dear Dad,*

*I was very pleased to get a letter from you. As far as I can remember it is the first, and this is the first time I have ever written to you.*

*Firstly, I should like to thank you for the present of £5 5s – naturally, I have already thanked mother – and I have the certificates in my book along with three others I had bought myself making a grand total of ten so I am not doing too badly.*

*Now that I have 'come of age' I should like to thank you for all the things you have done for me in my first 21 years of life. You have done everything in your power to give me a good start in life, and there is not another man I would liked to have had for a father than you. I know you have strived very hard to build a decent home for your wife and children to live in and – being in the Navy – I admire you very much for leaving drink alone and sending your money home… in that respect I am following you very closely, for, although I am nearly always mixing with people who like to drink, I have always refused to have* any myself, knowing that you would have been disappointed in me if I did.

Yes Dad, you and mother have looked after me well for 21 years, and as I have said before, you have made many sacrifices for the others and myself, and now it is up to me to look after myself and make sure that you and mother are never short of anything, and if there is ever anything at all that I can do for you, you can rest assured that I will do it.

I expect by now you will have heard that I passed my examination first class. Not bad eh? Well, that is the first rung of the ladder. One day I hope to be a lot nearer the top, for I still intend, when I get the chance, to carry on with my studies. Of course, this war has knocked everybody's ideas sky high, but when it is all over we can hope to settle down once again, for I feel certain we shall win.

Auntie Florrie and little Betty are, as you know, living with us now, and every one seems very happy. Auntie Florrie will prove to be a great help to mother, for it is hard work to look after us all alone.

Things are very quiet up here in the way of air

*raids but I've heard you've been catching it a bit down there.*

*Well Dad, mother is calling me for supper so I think I had better close, and wish you the best of luck always.*

*Your loving son,*

*Fred*

★   ★   ★

On 28 August 1941, Leslie Ford, who was the personal driver to the Squadron Leader commanding RAF Valley, attempted a brave rescue. When a Blackburn Botha aircraft crashed into rough seas at Rhosneigr Bay, Leslie and 11 others swam out to try to save the lives of the crew. But the conditions were horrendous, and they all drowned.

The following is an extract from *The History of RAF Valley*: 'Earlier in August, Valley had assumed responsibility for 2 air/sea rescue launches which were based at Rhoscolyn Bay close to the airfield; during that month, a tragic incident occurred in which the launches were unable to help when a Blackburn Botha (L6417) of No 4 Air Observers School from West Freugh force-landed in rough sea off Rhosneigr beach. The crew were drowned and so also were 11 other people including airmen from the Station who attempted in vain to rescue the crew and were lost when their boat capsized. Two young boys from Rhosneigr fearlessly put to sea in a sailing dinghy in an effort to reach the aircraft, but were unable to save the crew who were swept away by the towering waves which also overturned their little boat. They were fortunately rescued by the spectators on the beach who roped themselves together and waded out to them; for their bravery, the 2 boys were awarded the George Cross by the King.'

Later, his commanding officer wrote to Anne, Leslie's wife, saying that 'we all admire the pluck and courageous spirit shown by your husband in this gallant effort of his to save the lives of others. He was my personal driver and I felt he fully deserved promotion to a higher status in the Royal Air Force and had decided to recommend him for a commission.' He says Leslie was seen walking along the sands beforehand but that no one saw him enter the sea, although it was assumed that he had. He adds how popular he was, and that he was an excellent swimmer and it would have been typical of him just to have gone out there without saying a word to anyone. He pays a very appreciative tribute to Leslie.

Leslie wrote this last letter to his wife the day before he drowned. It shows his day-to-day concerns, which give fascinating insights into wartime existence, and also shares his eagerness to have photos of his beloved wife and his 'wee' son, Tony.

It sounds bizarre to hear him talking about playing tennis, then about 'two of the Boys' shooting down a Junkers 88, followed by his more mundane concerns and his desires to wear his grey suit and brown shoes. But that is the sort of ridiculous mix-up that war causes. It is also a very loving letter that his wife and son must have looked at many times after his sudden death.

He was due to see them in nine days' time; of course, sadly, he never made it.

*My Own Darling Anne*
*I expect I am in for an awful nagging for not writing sooner, but really darling I have been busy this last week with repairs and overhauls on the car. Yesterday afternoon was my first leisure period*

for a long time and I went into Bangor and played tennis. Well, my precious one, the time is drawing very close for my leave, and as far as I know it will be OK for Friday week, Sept 5th.

We had a Junkers 88 over here yesterday, but two of the Boys went up and shot it down, so that called for celebrations.

How is my dearest Anne and my 'Wee Man', is his cold better?

What about that film I put in the camera… have you taken any snaps with it yet? Don't forget, you must send me some.

I had a letter from Mum and they seem to be quite well, she sent me some stamps so I can write to you now even though it is just before pay day.

Have you been to Stoneleigh at all? If you go, do you think you could manage to convey my grey suit and a couple of shirts, collars and ties, also my brown shoes to Farnham so that I can change into them when I come on leave… please, darling.

You know, dearest, I keep getting so excited when I think of my leave 'cause I do so want to be with you and Tony. I keep showing people those two snaps that Hubert took and they all think Tony is a beautiful boy, it is so lovely to

*have him in the world with us, isn't it darling? I*
*don't know what I would do without my Anne*
*and Tony to love, and when I say love I mean*
*love… see?*

*Now precious Angel, I must away again so*
*cheerio darling, will write again soon.*

*Yours for evermore*
*Leslie xxxxxxxxx*
*xxxxxxxxxxxxxx*
*Tony xxxxxxxxxx*

★　　★　　★

Private C Royston Jones of the London
Regiment was in the civil service until he
volunteered to join the army in 1915 and went
to the front in October of that year. He was
involved in a lot of fighting and had some
narrow escapes, but on 15 September 1916, he
was killed taking a German trench during the
Battle of the Somme.

On 17 October 1916, his commander of
platoon writes to his father with the details of the
last moments 'of his heroic son'. He says, 'I knew
him as a keen and willing soldier, a straight man,
and a true friend. Such as he was to many of us.'

*Private C Royston Jones*

He writes about the morning when they mounted the trench parapet and waited for their orders to advance on the enemy's position. They rose together in one line, but the line became broken and Royston went off by himself. 'He saw, no doubt, soldier that he was, some chance that offered of striking a hard blow home.' But he was never seen alive again.

They found his body after their mission had been accomplished. 'We discovered his body, not long after we had finally captured our objective; surrounding him was enough evidence bearing testimony to a struggle having taken place. That is all we definitely know of a glorious end to a beautiful life.'

Roy's last letter is to his father and he wrote it a couple of days before he died. It shows a little of what life in the army was like during World War I and how precious letters and parcels from home were. As with other letters from that era, the reader can't help noticing the acute formality of his expressions and how distant the brutality of this war is from his words. By using this style of writing, the recipient is partially protected from the grim reality of war, and is encouraged to focus on the less upsetting subject areas, such as little luxury items like razor blades.

*Sunday 10th September*
*(On the Move)*
*France*

*Dear Father*

*Just a few lines to let you know I am quite in the 'pink' and to thank you for your last long letter, which I enjoyed very much. I have received everything sent including the last parcel (the contents, tell mother, were quite all right and had not been damaged).*

*When there is anything serious, I shall write every two days or so. We are at present out of line. The books you sent were very enjoyable. Please thank my sister for the photograph sent — I am writing separately when I have time. Hoping you are very well.*

*Yours sincerely*

*Roy*

*PS I want some safety razor blades as soon as poss, as I have run out of them. Also a new shirt. Many thanks by the way for all the attention to*

*my wants which you have given. I really can't
thank you enough and I am indeed very grateful.
Please give my love to mother.*

★　　★　　★

Lady Barlow of Wimpole St, London, provided a
letter from Private Basil Barlow, who was fighting
in the trenches in France during World War I
when he developed chronic trench foot. He is in
an army hospital in France and reports to his
father in other letters that 'poison had spread all
up the leg'. Six days before his last postcard, he
wrote a letter to his father talking about the
diagnosis on his foot. In fact, he initially had an
incorrect diagnosis at the clearing station but his
condition was eventually correctly identified as
trench foot. He describes 'fine incisions that were
made in his leg and two abcesses removed and a
tremendous amount of pus'. He'd also had a fever
and wasn't sleeping well.

In the same letter, he also says his leg is much
better after draining treatment, but that he's still
weak and uninterested in anything like books.
He also asks his father to stop sending
consultants – his father is presumably a

consultant himself – to see him, and that he has total confidence in his doctor there. The only thing Basil requests are some oranges. He also mentions that they are talking of sending him to England in a week's time.

However, by the time he writes his final postcard on 10 January 1917, his handwriting has deteriorated badly and he is obviously in a lot of pain. He died shortly afterwards.

His stoicism is amazing to behold. He sees no point in his parents coming to visit him. Basil is a spectacular example of an old-school soldier. The subtext of his postcard suggests immense pain and the dignity with which he is bearing it.

*Jan 10th 1917*

*Patience is required on my part to get through my daily trials. I must ask you to reciprocate and not get impatient at my not coming to England yet. The leg does go on alright – it was opened again yesterday and a deal of pus removed, I hope this really is the last. There is no swelling in the leg at all. Of course, it is difficult to find every pocket where matter may be lurking.*

118

When I do leave for England, we shall send a wire to Wimpole St giving the name of the boat and everything. I am still weak and personally do not think I shall be fit for travel for at least another week.

Please do not think of coming out, really there is no necessity. I do not want anything, except fruit.

Fondest love

PBB

COTTON TRADERS

BRU62

IRN BRU 62
BANK OF SCOT
PRST

REF NO
COTTON TRADERS
WEB02785178. INVOICE

# 5

## Death Draws Near for the Fatally Ill

Last letters from the fatally ill are simultaneously heartbreaking and inspiring. What is often striking is that the certainty of their death brings with it an acceptance. The constraint of death seems to lend the writer a freedom to inhabit the best of themselves.

It also presents them with the opportunity to reflect upon their love for their friends and families and find extraordinary ways of expressing it, sometimes utilising the simplest and most direct forms of expression.

When you have a young family and you are about to die prematurely, of course your thoughts turn to the future of your children and how you will miss their growing up. Some terminally ill mothers, like Anne Reid, chose to leave words of wisdom to help their children on their way to adulthood and to retain an influence on their lives.

Psychologists have realised that there are huge advantages for the family, especially the children, of the terminally ill if there are tangible memories set down in letters, videos, tapes, CDs, all of which can be accessed long into the future. Increasingly, people are talking about the psychotherapeutic value of memory boxes. Spoken words disappear, but written words last forever and are something to hold close to one's heart.

Thoughtful, loving, appreciative, kind — these letters are beautiful. And, in one case, a political act as well.

★   ★   ★

Eighty-year-old Harry Jones, a former bailiff from Leicester, had already had four operations for cancer. He was man with a great sense of humour despite his terrible illness — after one operation, he had to have his neck stapled, and thought it was very funny when his daughter referred to him as 'the son of Frankenstein'.

Not one to wear his heart on his sleeve, when he had to go in for his fifth operation in October 1994, he prepared himself for the worst possible outcome. Before the operation, he wrote a farewell letter and sealed it in an envelope, giving it to his wife Anne, but insisted that she only open it if he didn't come out of the operating theatre.

He survived that operation, but died on 2

*Harry Jones*

*Harry Jones*

January 1995, when Anne, who is 20 years younger than him, finally read his last letter.

'I found it very moving,' she says, 'because my husband was old school. He was a wonderful man and a great character who is spoken about with much affection by many people even 13 years later.' His last letter is a romantic goodbye, as well as a practical one. He makes sure he tells her where the deeds to the house are and points out how important the boundary line is!

*Dearest,*

*Who knows what tomorrow will bring? Whatever happens, I will love you always and be with you always.*

*Remember what I told you a while back: 'When you are near, the day is bright. When you are not, it's always night.' It may sound a little 'Mills and Boon' but it is true. When you go out and are overdue returning, I wonder what is the reason. Even your shopping visits in the village.*

*I count myself well blessed when I look at you and the Family.*

*That's all I have to say, not much but deeply felt.*

*Love, Joe*

127

*If things should turn out wrong – Fergus's debt is settled. Samantha has the Rocking Horse, a nice little job to finish. The child's stick back chair. The Water Colour of children fishing, I think it is in the Blue Room, and the china Ornaments in the Fireside cupboard. Brobyn the tools to finish the job.*

*All the rest is yours. Be careful.*

*The Deeds for the House are in the large tin Box in the Cupboard by the fireplace. Important plan shows the boundary line near the barn.*

★    ★    ★

Anne Reid was 33 years old in 1992 when she discovered she was dying of cervical cancer. Her children, Karl and Kandy, were two and one. Understandably, Anne was tormented with thoughts about what could happen to her children without their mother.

During a period of remission, Anne had an idea. She would get together a treasure chest or memory box for her children, which would contain information about her childhood and her life, as well as words of wisdom which would help them with their journeys into adulthood, including a last letter to them both. She even touchingly left them some of her perfume so they would know what their mother smelled like!

She also writes about what a shock the news of terminal cancer was to her. 'In life, unpredictable things happen that can completely alter the future. They can dash any hopes, dreams or ambitions one may have. In my case, just when I thought I had my whole life in front of me with two darlings and Daddy, I fell ill with cancer. I always thought we would have tomorrow, but now I'm not so sure…'

On finding out about her cancer, she describes it like a bomb that had been placed on her lap and was about to explode. At least, by making her treasure chest for her darling young sons, she did something sweet, courageous and creative to combat her cruel illness.

*My darlings Karl and Kandy,*

*By the time you read this, you will already know about the box of treasures I have left for you and, by now, you will also know why.*

*When I look back, I realise that I only*

discovered what living was all about when I had you two babies. Through the letters I have left for you in your treasure chest, you will learn that, for ages, I wasn't able to have children. I went to see several doctors, had some medical treatment and then, against the odds, you two were born. True to Murphy's Law, however, if anything can go wrong, it will. I had spent a lifetime searching for real happiness and then, when I found it, I learnt that I had also developed cancer. I was only 33. You, Karl, were only two years old, and Kandy was one.

My first thought was, what would happen to my babies? Who would look after you while you grew up; who would advise you after I had gone? And do it in the way that only a mother can?

You mean so much to me and I know I mean so much to you but, as I write this, I can't escape the fact that you are so young. By the time you become teenagers, I may be just a hazy memory. You might spend your lives wondering what your mother was really like. Was I good? Bad? Kind? Fair? Was I decadent or well principled? What were my beliefs? Did I have any at all? You would want to know all about your roots, all the things a simple photograph can't tell you.

*I spent many sleepless nights worrying about the things you'll need to know and the guidance you'll require throughout your lives. Then the answer came to me. It was so simple and obvious. I would look after you long after I had gone. I would tell you absolutely everything about yourselves and me and wouldn't leave a thing out, not even the things most people spend a lifetime trying to hide.*

*Some day, a teacher may ask what your mummy does for a living. You might reply that I passed away when you were small. The teacher might say, 'Oh, I'm sorry. Then you didn't know your mummy at all.' But you will be able to say, 'Oh, yes, Miss. I know her very well.'*

*Once I knew what I had to do, I set to thinking how to go about it and that's when I hit on the idea of the treasure chest.*

*It is filled with photographs and video tapes of Mummy and yourselves. There are Dictaphone tapes of Mummy's advice to you — a Dictaphone so that you have no excuse not to listen to them — memories, letters and the perfume I wear every day, so that you can remember what Mummy smelled like. There are legal documents and the* names of, and contact numbers for people who knew me during my life. I have even included a cotton hanky for each of you – wipe away your tears. The Dictaphone tape will be given to you at certain stages during your growing lives, because there are certain things that you may not be able to understand at too young an age.

Life is a never-ending series of falls and recoveries. You will make countless mistakes along the way but that is all a part of growing up. Most caring parents would do anything to stop their children from making the same mistakes that they did but, in my experience, although you can advise children not to do certain things, they will anyway. Even if I were alive, there is no guarantee you would heed warnings. I wouldn't dream of dictating to you how to lead your lives.

However, I can tell you what has happened in my life. You will learn that I had a lot of fun throughout the years – and more than my fair share of disasters. I did as many silly, foolish things as I did good. I'm sure some pennies will drop as you read the letters and listen to the tapes, for, by that time, you may have encountered similar incidents. You must make your own decisions *about how to deal with life's hurdles. I can only let you know how I dealt with mine and perhaps that will help you to help yourself. I hope that you will come to the best conclusions possible and make the right choices.*

*Most of all, by my leaving this treasure chest, you will know how much Mummy really, truly loved you. If it is possible still to feel love after one has gone, then, certainly, I will love you for all eternity, for you are the treasures in my life and I shall cherish you for all time.*

*All love,*

*Mummy xx*

★　　★　　★

Kay Milner decided to use her death as a protest against deaths without dignity. Her last letter to her friends makes her choices crystal clear. She is courageously making a stand in favour of right-to-die organisations and the wishes of the individual with regard to dignity and dying. She is using her last letter in a humanitarian way and to put the case for dying in the manner of one's own choosing. Kay belonged to Compassion and Choices, a non-profit organisation in Arizona, dedicated to making physician aid-in-dying a legally available option for terminally ill people.

It is a bold, brave last letter which is informing her friends and interested strangers that it is possible to confront terminal illness in this way – head on. She makes it clear that she did not want to suffer surgery or prolonged treatment and makes a valid case for choosing how you wish to die, but also making sure one's affairs are in order first.

*My Dear Friends*

*By the time you receive this letter I will be gone. Please read this letter knowing that I am doing what I want to do. Please don't feel regrets for me. It's my choice.*

*I was informed on June 10th 1997 that I had lung cancer. I consulted a pulmonary specialist, a thoracic surgeon and an oncologist. I had several chest X-rays, an extended breathing test and a lung biopsy, followed by conferences of radiologists and all other doctors. I was told that the cancer was of a fast-growing type and, even with major lung surgery and extensive, aggressive chemotherapy and radiation, the chances of survival were only about 20% for a two-year period, and even then I would be oxygen-*

*dependent for whatever time I had left to live. Faced with that grim prognosis, I immediately decided to have no surgery or treatment of any kind.*

*I have spent these last months getting my affairs in order and enjoying what few activities, events and friends that I was able to enjoy. My thinking for years has been that death was not to be feared but should be as quick and painless as possible. Hospice care facilities and hospitals were not to my liking, mainly because of legal restrictions, and consequently I supported the idea of self-deliverance and that is what I have done.*

*You might not agree with what I have done and you might not ever want to consider self-deliverance for yourself, but I hope you agree that I, and thousands of others in the same position as I was, should have the right of ending our lives as we wish to, without pain, debilitation, and suffering, and while we are still mentally and physically in control of our destinies.*

*I have enjoyed your company and friendship immensely. It has been a great satisfaction to me and I consider it a privilege to have known you.*

*Good-bye, my friends.*

*Affectionately, Kay*

\*　　\*　　\*

Novelist and journalist Melissa Nathan found out she had breast cancer when she was 33 in 2001. She wouldn't let this illness dominate her life and took a humorous view of its invasion of her body, she even joked about cancer's unoriginality in her column in the *Jewish Chronicle*. She wrote romantic comedies like *The Nanny* (2002) and *The Waitress* (2004) that were set in the world of work and very much for the post-feminist generation of women. They were bestsellers.

Born in 1968, she was a keen actress, studied Communications at the Polytechnic of Wales in Pontypridd, then did a postgraduate course in journalism at Cardiff University. She worked on magazines but her aspirations lay in novel-writing. Her first novel, *Pride, Prejudice and Jasmin Field* (2000) reworked Jane Austen in a modern setting and she used her acting experience to portray a group of amateurs putting on a play version of *Pride and Prejudice* – with Mr Darcy transformed into a celebrity actor. It was while working on her next book, *Persuading Annie* (2001), that Melissa discovered she had breast cancer.

*Melissa Nathan*

Melissa was witty and warm in person as well as in her books. So, in a way, it was no surprise that she chose to treat her cancer in a humorous, down-to-earth way as well. She refused to let the illness dominate her life and, in public, adopted a relentlessly positive attitude. She didn't like most of the journalism written by cancer sufferers because she found it self-indulgent and miserable. 'Self-indulgent dirges without a helpline in sight,' she said. She preferred laughing in adversity.

She feared the cancer would stop her becoming a mother but, after initial treatment went well, in March 2003 she gave birth to her son, Sam. However, not long afterwards, tests confirmed that cancer had spread to her liver, and Melissa had arduous cycles of treatment for it. Meanwhile, *The Nanny* climbed the bestseller charts and she continued work on *The Waitress*, even doing research in her local café. She did not want to allow the cancer to affect her daily activities.

However, despite her best efforts, the cancer could not be stopped.

She made a heroic effort to be at her son's third birthday party, and spent her final weeks finishing off her fifth novel, *The Learning Curve*, which was published four months before she died, and writing letters and stories for Sam to read when he was older. She used the opening pages of her last book as a final letter to her family and friends. She was very happily married to her husband, Andrew Saffron.

It's striking how she takes the opportunity to let her parents know that she is at peace with her illness, and the fact that she has had 37 wonderful years. From her words, you can tell how well supported and loved she was as a person. To her husband, she is able to say that she respects him as well as loves him, then acknowledges what a big deal that is for her. She pays homage to their 12 years of marriage in a typically self-deprecating way, then goes on to leave words of total adoration to her three-year-old son, Sammy. Her final words are a testament to her generosity as a human being.

*I am in the unusual position of knowing that this book will, in all probability, be published posthumously. And so please indulge me in a rather unusual set of acknowledgements.*

*First, to my wonderful parents. You have given me a life suffused with love, support and friendship. I have been lucky enough to see eye to*

139

eye with you both and look up to you at the same time. You are two of my best friends. Please never feel that I have had a hard life. I have had 37 wonderful years and I'm grateful to you both for giving me that. I am happy and at peace.

To Jeremy. It turned out that our dynamic was to be that of doctor and patient. I would never have chosen it to be that way, but there it was. You were always there for me, from the first phone call I made when I was 19, telling you I'd found a lump, right through to — and beyond — the night you stayed in hospital with me, sleeping on an inflatable lilo on the floor, when I had my first mastectomy some 17 years later. You have been everything a brother could have been and more. Thank you.

My wonderful Andrew. I respect you as much as I love you, and that is saying something. You, of all people I know, will get through this. After all, you've got through nearly 12 years of marriage with me and that's no easy feat. I have been so lucky to know you. You have been my steady rock, my gentle giant, my best friend, my everything. I wish you a happy life, full of love and joy.

And my amazing Sammy. I wanted to know

*you for longer, my love, but it wasn't to be. Still, at only three years old, you have already left an imprint on my heart that will go with me, wherever it is I'm going. Motherhood made my life worthwhile. And you gave me that. What does a mother wish for her son? I wish you happiness. You have a wonderful daddy and a family who adores you. Go into the world knowing that while you were everything to your mother, you won't have to deal with an annoying woman who can't stop kissing you when you're 15. I will be in the sky kissing you from afar.*

*Lots of love*
*Melissa*

melissanathan.com is where you will find details of the Melissa Nathan Foundation.

# 6

*Suicide Notes*

Is there a typical suicide note? The experts would probably say yes and no. The Forensic Linguistic Institute in Wales analysed a suicide note from someone who jumped under a train. It is typical in that it is short – 78 words – and it expresses pain and regret as well as resignation and guilt:

*I have looked at our 18 years mainly as happy years and had hoped to spend old age together.*

*Surely, my exaggerated attitude towards work has brought you sorrow and loneliness.*

*I wanted the best for all of you and, looking back, I too made some sacrifices. That the children suffered from this, I can now see.*

*I hope you can forgive me, I just can't carry on, the despair is too great.*

Obviously written to his wife, there is a feeling that he has somehow not been respected for all that he thinks he has given and 'sacrificed'. He also suggests some anger over his despairing predicament.

The brother of a friend of mine also killed himself, and my friend cannot bear this act to be described as 'committing suicide', because using the verb 'commit' implies that this was a sinful action. I agree that suicide should not be tainted by this kind of religious overtone. Christianity dictated that people who 'committed' suicide were criminals. That created a taboo around suicide that is not so strong today, but still exists in a shadowy, more subtle form. There is still a great deal of shame attached to it, and it still generally remains a taboo topic of conversation, particularly if a family has been touched by it.

Understanding why people kill themselves is an important endeavour. Suicide notes help, although they are mostly written in moments of utter hopelessness. The exception is 'sane' suicides – for instance, where someone is fatally ill, and so has made a conscious, considered decision that their quality of life is severely impaired and, therefore, they wish to control the manner of ending it. In my opinion, in a mature society, suicide is an option, which should be open to everyone.

Some people who kill themselves manage to retain a generosity of spirit and want to make sure no one else blames themselves; others are simply in too much mental anguish and want revenge; others are far, far too young to be contemplating such an act but their despair leads them to it. Above all, suicide notes tell society a story that should be listened to.

The anonymous notes in this section are German.

★   ★   ★

Zoe Schwarz killed herself on 22 August 2000. She was 27 and she left a note primarily to say that no one was to blame. However, the subtext was that she didn't feel anything could be done about her unbearable depression. She couldn't see any other escape.

Zoe was bipolar, which meant her life was divided dramatically into ups and downs. One in five people who are bipolar eventually commit suicide. 'Bipolar affective disorder', as manic depression is now termed, has been associated down the ages with charisma and creativity – Byron, Coleridge, Melville, Graham Greene, Virginia Woolf, Strindberg, Spike Milligan, Vivien Leigh and Kurt Cobain were all reported to be sufferers as have been Stephen Fry and Francis Ford Coppola.

Zoe's first bipolar episode happened when she

*Zoe Schwarz*

was 18 just after a bout of glandular fever, and before she went off to Bristol University. She was manic – as in wild, aggressive and promiscuous – and she was thrown out. She was then depressed and took an overdose. Aided by some drugs and counselling, she recovered, to the extent that she returned to complete her course and gained an MSc.

Her family didn't realise for a long time that she was bipolar. They simply thought that her behaviour was eccentric, due to her strong and dramatic personality. Zoe was intelligent and vivacious. She had a great job at United Response, a large charity, where she was hugely appreciated. She began smoking marijuana and then went off to stay in Morocco indefinitely. She became crazy. Her parents ended up having her sectioned in a secure mental hospital in Marrakesh. They eventually managed to repatriate her within 12 days with the help of the British consul.

Then she became depressed again, and this state continued for some time. She became immobilised. Drugs and therapy didn't work. She was desperate, and so were her parents. They regretted not hugging her more, although the psychiatrist had advised them to leave her alone.

On 21 August 2000, it was decided by a psychiatrist that she should be admitted to hospital and that a new strategy should commence. The next day, she threw herself into the speeding path of an express train.

She had planned her death quite meticulously – having left her car at a station in Essex, she hid behind a pillar on the platform and then threw herself high in the air into the path of the driver's cab of the London express which was hurtling down the track. This was a determined act of suicide. Poor Zoe, who was talented and charismatic and lived life to the full, couldn't take any more of her illness. She'd been depressed for four months and she felt as though she was living behind a glass wall. Beautiful, gifted Zoe was dead.

Her parents, Dorothy and Walter, feel they should not have kidded themselves that she would recover when she was ready. They wish they had acted more effectively to secure her treatment sooner. 'If only, while she was such a bundle of morosity and self-absorption, we had kissed her more often,' they said later. They would like to urge other loving relatives of bipolar sufferers to act sooner.

*To my family and friends and Hicham [Hicham is her Moroccan lover]*

*No one is to blame for my death. I am killing myself because the circumstances of my life are unbearable. I love you all; but I can't live like this. I am in too much pain and I am just deteriorating. I'm sorry, please forgive me.*

*I used to work and see friends a lot; but now I can do neither because I can't function or communicate. I've been in hell for four months and I can't bear the pain any more.*

*Zoe*

★　　★　　★

W's marriage had ended and his wife had moved in with her new lover. W couldn't accept this situation. He offered ultimatums and threatened violence against the lover, and, finally, W visited the family home when he knew his four children were at school and his former wife was in. They apparently had an argument in the kitchen and

W hit his ex-wife with a hammer on the back of the head. He wrote a bitter but also anguished suicide note to his rival, then locked the kitchen door. He was a very angry man. Taking the key with him, he went straight to the local railway station and threw himself under a train.

This suicide note shows someone who cannot get over losing his wife to someone else. It is full of revenge and bitterness, and suggests a mind that has obviously tipped into insanity. W's grief at the loss of not just his wife, but also his children and his flat, has made him demented with rage. He repeats his resentment again and again. This is a man driven to insanity, to the extent that he 'bestows' his four children into the care of his enemy, his wife's lover. Finally, he implores the man he hates to look after his children when he's gone. It's a terrible, painful tragedy.

*Dear Mr S*

*Today is the day of reckoning for what you have done to me and my wife. I've suffered a lot during this year since the divorce. I can't bear to look at the terrible things you have done to me* any more. 14 years I worked and she got the lot, the whole lot. I didn't even get a bed. That's the thanks I got for 14 years' work. She's getting her thanks back today. My car's sold, and the money is to be put in my kids' savings accounts in equal shares.

Please don't dump my kids the way you dumped your own.

So you've got my whole household now, just see how you cope with that. Your wife will be delighted but she won't take you back. The year since the divorce has driven me crazy. I don't know what I'm doing any more. But I'm not ending up in prison because of you, that'd be too big a price to pay for that slag. It's been an awful time for me. I've not been able to sleep at night for months. I don't have any choice.

Yes, you're going to be punished for your bad behaviour now. I pulled my four kids out of the gutter and the thanks I get for that is paying child support without even being allowed to see my own children. It didn't have to be like this. I was good for 14 years and now all of a sudden I'm just shit. You've got my whole household now just see how you cope with it. If you dump my kids nothing at all belongs to you, it's all the children's. I loved my kids, that's why they're to get the money for the car. Whoever's interested in my tools can have them, I haven't got anything else. My parents have got the log book. I'd have died of misery anyway, it was all her fault.

During the divorce I gave her my whole end of year bonus and the thanks I got was having to pay for the court and the lawyer. It was a terrible time. She wanted the car as well, tax, insurance, child support, rent a garage, even though I built it with my own hands. That really pissed me off. I'm ashamed because of my children but I don't have any choice. If her mother was still alive, it wouldn't have come to this. If she hadn't cast me in such a bad light maybe it wouldn't have come to this. It's done my head in, I don't know if I'm still quite normal, that's what it's all done to me. Now you've got your punishment for what you did to your wife and your 3 kids.

I gave her a year to come back to me — that time has already passed but now it's over. I'm not too cowardly to throw myself under a train but I'm not going to prison. She's not worth it. If you dump my kids the place is yours, including the *bedroom suite, and my car. But please don't dump my kids. Cos all this whoring about, it's not their fault. They don't deserve it any different. Your wife will be pleased and I'm punishing my slag something terrible. I made a nice nest for my kids. I can't do anything else for them now. If she'd given me just the bare essentials I might have got over it but not even so much as my duvet.*

*Now here is my grizzly thanks for what you vile people have done to me.*

★   ★   ★

Thirteen-year-old Vijay Singh from Lancashire hanged himself in 1996 because he had been persistently bullied. His last note is hauntingly simple and informative about the cruelty he had been suffering. His words are simply unforgettable.

*I shall remember forever and will never forget*
*Monday; my money was taken.*
*Tuesday; named called.*
*Wednesday; my uniform torn.*
*Thursday; my body pouring with blood.*
*Friday; it's ended.*
*Saturday; freedom.*

On Sunday, he was found hanging from a banister rail at his home. Tragically, his mother, Hardev, didn't realise how bad the bullying was, because her son wasn't able to tell her. Typically, he was too scared and ashamed. Twelve years later, she still misses him terribly. 'As time goes by, it gets worse and worse,' she says, 'there are all these occasions like Valentine's which are about love, and which bring back everything I have lost. He was so precious to me.'

***

One day in June, a husband arrived home to discover his wife in their bed wearing a red-and-black summer dress. She was dead.

At first, it seemed absurd that she had taken her life. She didn't have a child and she wanted at least one, but her husband didn't think this was the reason for her suicide. She had cried from time to time but he'd never known why. She'd had two miscarriages but some thought she might be pregnant.

U had left a package alongside her suicide note. The note read: 'His Hamilton syringe is in the packet along with a book and a present he gave me that I never liked. Please inform Dr L.'

U had been having an affair with 'Dr L', who was married with two children. Notes were found around the flat which explained that Dr L knew that her difficulties getting pregnant originated from sexual abuse by her father. U obviously could find no simple way out of her complicated situation, so she killed herself. Her post-script instructions also tell the tale of a woman who was particular about appearances. They are curious details in a suicide note.

It is full of self-pity, blame and anger. U felt abandoned by everyone and she couldn't face her life any longer.

*Right up to the very last, you get no consideration from me – I'm terribly sorry – please forgive me. I've lost my grip.*

*Even your guiding principle – that the will just needs to be there – made me feel even more desperate.*

*I've always admired you and held you in high regard. You're a unique person, and you've always helped me. But now you couldn't help me any* more. I know you're strong enough to go your own way without me.

I was always a misfit in this world.

I've been a real burden to you, especially over these last six months, because I've known for six months what I was going to do.

I owe you an explanation, too.

Someone called Dr L had me completely under his sway.

I was like a piece of paper that he could crumple up and flatten out, and then crumple up again. I've tried to find some stability with you, but I just couldn't manage it any more.

Please don't go looking for Dr L, and don't let him come looking for you. He's completely inhuman. You're human. I don't want him to be there on that dreadful day either.

Please forgive me. I couldn't think of any alternative.

U

Please: no white shirt.

My black dress and camel coat.

Twenty-two-year-old K suffered from depression. She had a two-year-old son but her relationships with men were not working out. Her marriage had lasted two years. She had a fiancé, G, but something didn't seem right with this relationship either.

On the night of her death, she allowed a pilot she had known vaguely for years to accompany her home. Presumably, he innocently thought he was in for a good time. However, later on, she sealed her son's bedroom door with tape, and left a note saying 'please save my son', and turned the gas taps on the cooker full on. K and the pilot died. Her father discovered them both the next day — she lay next to the cooker in her underwear, he was naked on the sofa. She wrote a desperate suicide note to her mother.

*My dear mum, my only dear mum,*

*I'm sorry, but it's my same old pain again!*

*Leave me in peace, I've been searching for it for ages.*

*Life is hell, just meaningless, nobody understood me.*

*I couldn't go on living.*

*At last, I'm experiencing death, life was terrible.*

*Life is just pain and bad luck, it hurts.*

*I didn't want to be disappointed yet again.*

*What's happened this evening is all just coincidence!*

*I love only G to my very last breath.*

*Please tell G that I loved him, it's revenge for F.*

*Forgive me, G.*

*Forgive me for taking a promising young pilot with me, dying's easier when there are two of you.*

*I tried to forget everything, even today.*

*Please tell G I really loved him, he never understood me!*

*I can't feel the gas any more, sorry…*

*Goodbye G! I loved you! My darling G! Please forgive me! The man lying next to me is just an unfortunate coincidence, both of us gassed, want to pray to God. Save my child. Bury me next to Daddy! Life is dreadful, please forgive me.*

★   ★   ★

Should you or anyone you know want help or advice on the subject of suicide, please contact the Samaritans helpline: 08457 909090.

# 7
## Final Words
## from Prisoners

Prisoners who are about to be executed have the opportunity, like all the other last-letter writers, to decide what is important enough to be articulated at this moment.

Some, like the US prisoners on Death Row, may feel wronged and that the system is unjust – although we should always be careful of trusting these last words – while others may want to ask for forgiveness and tell their families how much they love them. It's also hard when reading their last statements not to be aware of the enormity of the social disadvantage that some have suffered. That doesn't make their actions acceptable, but it is something that shouldn't be ignored.

On the other hand, political prisoners, like Patrick H Pearse, have been executed while still entirely committed to their principles and beliefs. They are dying for a higher cause, for a belief system that they are convinced is the only one worth following. Consequently, they can be eloquent in their last letters.

Finally, Harriet Parker, writing towards the end of the 19th century, obviously suffered some sort of mental breakdown. She was so jealous when her lover ran off with someone else that she was driven to murder his children. Her suicide note is a bitter explanation, while she also bizarrely requests that he pay off her debts.

★   ★   ★

Thirty-two-year-old Johnny Conner was holding up a shop in Houston, Texas, when a male customer tried to stop him. The customer was shot in the arm and chest but, as Conner fled, he also fatally shot a woman shop assistant in the head. He had no previous convictions. He was executed on 22 August 2007.

*Could you please tell that lady right there, can I see her, she is not looking at me. I want you to understand something, hold no animosity towards me. I want you to understand, please forgive me. When I get to the gates of heaven, I will open my arms for you. Please forgive me, do not worry about what is going to happen. I don't want you to worry. I don't want you to suffer, I am not mad at you. Shed no tears for me. Even though you don't know me, I love you, I love all of ya'll. I ask ya'll in your heart to forgive me.*

*To my family, I love all of you. What's happening now, you are suffering. I didn't mean to hurt you. Stephanie, Felicia, Carlos and my Father. I love my Father. I want you to understand that life goes on. Continue to live your life and don't be angry at what is happening to me. This is destiny, this is life. This is something I have to do and I am going to be with my momma and your momma. I want everyone to continue to live your life. Thank you and I love all of you.*

*What is happening to me now is unjust and the system is broken. At the same time, I bear witness there is no God but Allah and the Prophet Mohammad. Unto Allah, I belong, unto Allah I return. I love you.*

★   ★   ★

Thirty-nine-year-old, Patrick Knight was convicted in 1991 of the abduction and murders of Walter and Mary Werner of Amarillo. He was their neighbour and, according to relatives, had been harassing them. On the day of the crime, Knight and his accomplices broke into the Werners' home and waited for them to return. He held them captive there before driving them to a secret location and killing them. He was executed on 26 June 2007.

*I thank the Lord for giving me my friends, for getting me the ones I love. Lord, reach down and help innocent men on Death Row. Lee Taylor needs help, Bobby Hines, Steve Woods. Not all of us are innocent, but those are. Cleve Foster needs help.*

*Melyssa, I love you girl. I know I wasn't going to say anything, but I've got to. Jack, Irene, Danny, Doreen, I love you guys. I said I was going to tell a joke. Death has set me free. That's the biggest joke, I deserve this. And the other joke is I am not Patrick Bryan Knight, and ya'll can't stop this execution now. Go ahead, I'm finished. Come on, tell me Lord. I love you Melyssa, take care of that little monster for me.*

★   ★   ★

Thirty-seven-year-old Patrick H Pearse was imprisoned in Kilmainham Prison, Dublin. Teacher, barrister, poet and political activist, he was a nationalist. He wrote to his dear mother, letting her know he was ready to die. He was tried by

*Patrick H.Pearse*

Court Martial and shot the next day for his role as director of operations in the Dublin Easter Uprising in 1916. While World War I raged on the European mainland, the Easter Uprising paved the way for the 1918 election in which Sinn Fein was given a mandate to form an independent Irish parliament.

St Enda's was the bi–lingual school that Pearse started in the belief that Gaelic should not be lost as a language.

*My dearest Mother*

*I have been hoping up to now that it would be possible to see you again, but it does not seem possible. Goodbye, my dear, dear Mother. Through you, I say goodbye to Bow-wow, MB, Miss Myrne, Michael, Cousin Maggie and everyone at St Enda's. I hope and believe that Willie and St Enda's boys will be safe.*

*I have written two papers about Financial*

Affairs, and one about my books, which I want you to get. With them are a few poems, which I want added to the poems of mine in manuscript in the large bookcase.

You asked me to write a little poem which would seem to be said by you about me. I have written it and one copy is at Arbour Hill Barracks with the other papers. Fr Aloysius is taking charge of another copy.

I have just received Holy Communion and am happy except for the great grief of parting with you. This is the death I should have asked for if God had given me the choice of all deaths – to die a soldier's death for Ireland and for Freedom. WE HAVE DONE RIGHT, PEOPLE WILL SAY HARD THINGS OF US NOW, BUT LATER ON THEY WILL PRAISE US.

Do not grieve for all this, but think of it as a sacrifice, which God asked of me and of you. Goodbye again, dear, dear, Mother. May God bless you for your great love for me, and for your great faith, and may he remember all you have so bravely suffered. I hope soon to see Papa, and in a little while we shall all be together again. Bow-wow, Willie, M., Brigid and Mother, goodbye.

*I have no words to tell you of my love for you, and
how my heart yearns to you all. I will call to you
in my heart at the last moment.*

   *Your loving son,*

   *Pat*

A Mother Speaks

   Dear Mary that did'st see thy first-born
son go forth

   To die amidst the scorn of men for whom
he died;

   Receive my first-born son into thy arms,

   Who also had gone forth to die for men,

   And keep him by Thee til I come to him,

   Dear Mary I have shared thy sorrow, and
soon shall

   Share thy joy.

                 *P.H. Pearse, May 1916*

★   ★   ★

Harriet Parker was hanged at Newgate in 1848.
On the eve of her hanging, she wrote a letter to
her lover. Robert Blake had been married when
Harriet fell for him and, true to his womanising
form, as soon as they were together, he had an

affair with someone else. Harriet was so enraged that she committed a terrible crime – she suffocated Blake's two young children, who were four and six, just to get back at their father. She wrote Blake a last letter before her death.

*Dear Robert,*

*This is the last time you will ever receive advice from me. My days are numbered: this day fortnight I shall be silent in the grave. Take therefore these few lines into consideration: never again trifle with a woman as you have with me. Promise to forsake all others, and cling once again to her who ought to hold the only place in your heart – the wife of your bosom. This, Robert, I sincerely wish. I have deeply injured her, and so have you. Let her then, after this, have your best and purest affections.*

*Oh, Robert, had we parted long since, as I requested, my life, and that of those who were so near and dear to you, would have been spared… oh! May we yet meet in that land in which sorrow and misery will flee away. I only ask that you will sometimes shed the tear of pity and forgiveness over my unfortunate lot.*

170

*I wish you to pay some little debts for me, and I shall die much happier if you will. I owe the milk-woman 8d. Bridget did one half-day's work for me; and likewise Mrs Washington a trifle; and the greengrocer, for coals, I think about 2s 6d.*

*Now Robert, I must conclude; that God in mercy may forgive, bless, and prosper you and yours, is the sincere prayer of the heart that dictates these lines. From the unfortunate*

   *Harriet Parker*

# 8
## Famous Last Letters

The writers here are all well known now or historically – some better than others. Virginia Woolf, Captain Scott, Hunter S Thompson and Kurt Cobain still reign high in the visibility stakes, while others have faded from view. Ruth Ellis was infamous for being the last woman in Britain to be hanged, while the Rosenbergs were famous for being spies during the Cold War era. Wendy O Williams was famous on the music scene in the late 1970s and early 1980s, while Timothy Treadwell became famous because of Werner Herzog's film about his life, *Grizzly Man*, which was released in 2005.

What unites them – be they suicide notes, last letters from the fatally ill or letters prior to execution – is the drama of their writing. Hunter S Thompson is characteristically witty and resigned; Kurt Cobain vacillates between introspection and devotion; Ruth Ellis is pragmatic; Baden Powell is religiously righteous; Captain Scott is heroic; and the Rosenbergs are tragically sad when addressing their children. Dr Thomas Hodgkin was so ill that he had to dictate his last letter, while Wilfred Owen was under the impression that the war was almost over. However, it is the now little-known Hollywood actress Clara Blandick who exits with the most flamboyant flourish – 'I am going to make the great adventure'. They all are.

★   ★   ★

Sixty-seven-year-old Hunter S Thompson's suicide is almost as famous as his quintessentially excessive 'gonzo' novel *Fear and Loathing in Las Vegas*. Always reclusive, he lived with his much younger wife in Woody Creek, Colorado. On 20 February 2006, this literary anti-hero shot himself in the head. He was standing in the kitchen at the time, talking on the phone to his wife, Anita. His son and grandson were also in the house. His suicide note had been written to his wife four days earlier. It was brief and to the point, and humorous as well. Basically, he did not want to experience any more of the inconveniences of old age, like health problems. At his funeral, his ashes were fired into the air by a rocket, just as Hunter wanted. Funnily enough, he was an avid football fan.

*Hunter S Thompson*

*Football Season Is Over*

*No more games. No more bombs. No more walking. No more fun. No more swimming. 67. That is 17 years past 50. 17 more than I needed or wanted. Boring. I am always bitchy. No fun… for anybody. 67. You are getting greedy. Act your old age. Relax. This won't hurt.*

★   ★   ★

Forty-six-year-old Timothy Treadwell was killed and then eaten by a brown bear in Katmai National Park in Alaska on 5 October 2003. His girlfriend, Anne Huguenard, was killed and eaten as well. Timothy was an aspiring actor, a recovering alcoholic and drug addict, and an eco-warrior as well. He had spent 13 seasons living and filming the native brown bears, and had become something of a celebrity and controversial figure in the US because of his eagerness to live so closely to these magnificent creatures. Many experts disagreed with what they thought was a cavalier and dangerous attitude to the bears. However, he filmed over a hundred hours of amazing footage, some of which was used in a 2005 Werner Herzog documentary about his life;

*Timothy Treadwell*

his supporters think his work with the bears was invaluable.

One of his financial supporters was Ron Dixon, a rancher and conservation activist from Colorado. In late July, Timothy had arrived in the area he called the Grizzly Maze, the vast tangle of meadows and thickets stretching inland from Kaflia Bay. To his delight, the bears were faring well, particularly the one he called Aunt Melissa and her two cubs, Lily and Dixon.

Timothy had already written to Ron Dixon (he named the cub after his sponsor) on 25 August, believing he was experiencing a breakthrough. 'I am in the most exciting and dangerous time of my fieldwork. I am so deep within the brown bear culture. It is fascinating, beautiful and at times treacherous.'

This is his last letter to Ron Dixon before his death and was flown out on a bush plane carrying supplies. He managed to live extremely closely to these bears for 13 seasons but he was also dangerously deluded about his role; he believed that he had become accepted by the bears as one of them. He hadn't.

*Roland*

Hello! I am writing you a last letter for the journey. My last food delivery is scheduled for late today.

My transformation is complete – a fully accepted wild animal – brother to these bears. I run free among them – with absolute love and respect for all the animals. I am kind and viciously tough.

People – especially the bear experts of Alaska – believe this cannot be done. Some even bet on my death. They are sure you must have some sort of weapon for defense – pepper spray at the least, an electric fence a must. And you cannot hope to make it in a flimsy tent under thick cover among one of Earth's largest gatherings of giant brown grizzly bears.

People who knowingly enter bear habitat with pepper spray, guns and electric fences are committing a crime to the animals. They begin with the accepted idea of bringing instruments of pain to the animals. If they are that fearful, then they have no place in the land of this perfect animal.

Could I look at Dixon, Lily and their mother,

*Melissa, and tell them that I love them, that I will care for them, with a can of mace in my pocket? Does the fox or vole get zapped by the wicked sting of an electric fence for being curious?*

*This wilderness — the Grizzly Maze — had big problems not too many years ago. People who came to kill the animals. I was threatened with death. One group promising to stuff me alive in a crab pot and submerge it in the icy sea.*

*They are gone now. The Maze returned to the animals.*

*You made this possible. I am a miserable fundraiser. Without you, these animals would have been left without any care. Care that I can offer them, without any displacement or disrespect. I even erase my footprints.*

*You got me here for so many years. I will always remember and be thankful. I will tell [the bears] of your kindness and generosity. Animals alive because of you. Myself included.*

*Sincerely,*

*Timothy Treadwell*

*Wendy O Williams*

★　　★　　★

Forty-eight-year-old Wendy O Williams, lead singer of the seminal punk-metal band, Plasmatics, killed herself on 6 April 1998. She shot herself in the head. The Plasmatics became famous in the 1970s for their aggressive style of music and on-stage theatrics. Wendy would regularly chainsaw guitars, and speaker cabinets would detonate. She became known as the Queen of Shock Rock.

A native New Yorker, by 1998 she had been living with her manager, Rod Swenson, for more than 20 years, and they had moved to Connecticut. When he returned home that day, he discovered a package that Wendy had left for him which included special noodles that he liked, seeds for the garden, some oriental massage balm and sealed letters from her. These consisted of one which was a Living Will, refusing any life support, a love letter to him and lists of things to do, which prompted him to search the woods near their home.

He found her body in woods near an area where she loved to feed the wildlife. Several nuts were on the ground and she had apparently been feeding squirrels before she died. He said later that Wendy's death was not an irrational, spontaneous act; she had apparently been talking about taking her own life for about four years. She had enjoyed living in the world when she was at the peak of her career, but didn't want to live in it when her star began to wane.

He said, 'Speaking personally for myself, I loved her beyond imagination. She was a source of strength, inspiration and courage. The pain at this moment in losing her is inexpressible. I can hardly imagine a world without Wendy Williams in it. For me, such a world is profoundly diminished.'

Her Living Will suicide note read:

*The act of taking my own life is not something I am doing without a lot of thought. I don't believe that people should take their own lives without deep and thoughtful reflection over a considerable period of time. I do believe strongly, however, that the right to do so is one of the most fundamental rights that anyone in a free society should have. For me, much of the world makes no sense, but my feelings about what I am doing ring loud and clear to an inner ear and a place where there is no self, only calm.*

*Love always, Wendy*

★　　★　　★

Another legendary suicide was 27-year-old Kurt Cobain, lead singer of the band Nirvana, husband of the rock chick of all rock chicks, Courtney Love, and father of Frances Bean Cobain. He was an icon to many in the music world during his brief life as a rock star – he has since become a legend as a result of his untimely death.

Cobain was bipolar. On 8 April 1994, after he'd been missing for a few days, he was found dead at his home in Seattle; he'd shot himself in the head. He had struggled with depression and heroin addiction for years, and this was the end of his torment. On 10 April, 7,000 fans gathered to pay tribute to him in his local park; Love read out some of his suicide note and handed out remnants of his clothing.

His suicide note is lengthy. It's also pretentious, rambling and weirdly grandiose. He also utters the totally rock 'n' roll sentiment: 'it's better to burn out than fade away'.

*Kurt Cobain*

*To Boddah [Cobain's imaginary childhood friend]*

Speaking from the tongue of an experienced simpleton who obviously would rather be an emasculated, infantile complainee. This note should be pretty easy to understand.

All the warnings of the punk rock 101 courses over the years, since my first introduction to the, shall we say, ethics involved with independence and the embracement of your community has proven to be very true. I haven't felt the excitement of listening to as well as creating music along with reading and writing for too many years now, I feel guilty beyond words about these things.

For example, when we're back stage and the lights go out and the manic roar of the crowd begins, it doesn't affect me the way in which it did for Freddie Mercury, who seemed to love, relish in the love and adoration from the crowd which is something I totally admire and envy. The fact is, I can't fool you, any one of you. It simply isn't fair to you or me. The worst crime I can think of would be to rip people off by faking it and pretending as if I'm having 100% fun. Sometimes I feel as if I should have a punch-in time clock before I walk out on stage. I've tried *everything within my power to appreciate it (and I do, God, believe me, I do, but it's not enough). I appreciate the fact that I and we have affected and entertained a lot of people. I must be one of those narcissists who only appreciate things when they're alone. I'm too sensitive. I need to be slightly numb in order to regain the enthusiasms I once had as a child.*

*On our last 3 tours, I've had a much better appreciation for all the people I've known personally and as fans of our music, but I still can't get over the frustration, the guilt and empathy I have for everyone. There's good in all of us and I think I simply love people too much, so much that it makes me feel too fucking sad. The sad, little, sensitive, unappreciative, Pisces, Jesus man. Why don't you just enjoy it? I don't know!*

*I have a goddess of a wife who sweats ambition and empathy and a daughter who reminds me too much of what I used to be, full of love and joy, kissing every person she meets because everyone is good and will do her no harm. And that terrifies me to the point to where I can barely function. I can't stand the thought of Frances becoming the miserable, self-destructive, death rocker that I've become.*

189

*I have it good, very good and I'm grateful, but since the age of seven, I've become hateful towards all humans in general. Only because it seems so easy for people to get along that have empathy. Only because I love and feel sorry for people too much I guess.*

*Thank you all from the pit of my burning, nauseous stomach for your letters and concern during the past years. I'm too much of an erratic, moody baby! I don't have the passion any more, and so remember, it's better to burn out than to fade away.*

*Peace, love, empathy.*

*Kurt Cobain*


*Frances and Courtney, I'll be at your altar.*

*Please keep going Courtney, for Frances. For her life, which will be so much happier without me.*

*I LOVE YOU, I LOVE YOU!*

★　★　★

Eighty-two-year-old actress, Clara Blandick, whose most enduring role was as Auntie in *The Wizard of Oz*, was becoming blind and crippled with arthritis. On 15 April 1962, she returned from church and began rearranging rooms,

*Clara Blandick*

putting her favourite photos and possessions in visible places. They included her press clippings and a resumé of her life. She prepared herself for death immaculately. She put on an elegant blue dressing gown and made her hair look good, then she took an overdose of sleeping pills. Finally, she lay down on a couch, covered her shoulders with a gold blanket then tied a plastic bag over her head. She left a short suicide note.

*I am now about to make the great adventure. I cannot endure this agonising pain any longer. It is all over my body. Neither can I face the impending blindness. I pray the Lord my soul to take.*
*Amen*

★　　★　　★

Twenty-eight-year-old Ruth Ellis was the last woman to be hanged in Britain on 13 July 1955. She was accused of murdering David Blakely, her lover. They had a violent, jealousy-fuelled relationship and Ruth had already had a miscarriage which happened shortly after Blakely had hit her in the stomach, although she was reluctant to blame him.

*Ruth Ellis*

However, the Conservative British Home Secretary, Lloyd George, had ruled against a reprieve on 11 July. On 26 May, there had been an election; had the Labour Party formed the Government, her sentence would probably have been commuted to life imprisonment, which meant a maximum sentence of 12 years. But fate did not turn in that direction.

Ruth got up early on the last morning of her life and wrote letters of farewell. One was to Leon Simmons, the solicitor's clerk who had represented her in her divorce. He was the only lawyer she trusted, and she had met up with him to discuss her four-year-old daughter Georgina's welfare.

*Dear Mr Simmons,*
*The time is 7.00am. Everyone is simply wonderful in Holloway. This is just for you to console my family with the thought that I did not change my way of thinking at the last moment. Or break my promise to David's mother.* [In a previous letter to Mrs Cook, Ruth had confirmed her acceptance of an eye-for-an-eye, and was resigned to die so that his death could be repaid in some way.]

*Well, Mr Simmons, I have told the truth, and that's all I can do. Thanks once again,*
*Goodbye,*
*Ruth*

★ ★ ★

On 19 June 1953, 35-year-old Julius and 38-year-old Ethel Rosenberg were executed via electric chair after they had been convicted of conspiring to give atomic secrets to the Soviets.

*Julius and Ethel Rosenberg*

They were American Communists. From the time of their arrest to their execution, which spanned just over two years, they communicated regularly with their children, Michael, seven, and Robert, three. The Rosenbergs' refusal to talk and their staunch silence when it came to naming names resulted in their deaths – but they maintained their innocence to the end. They were the only two American citizens to be executed for espionage-related activities during the Cold War. This is the last letter that Ethel wrote to her sons.

*Dearest Sweethearts, my most precious children,*

*Only this morning it looked like we might be together again after all. Now that this cannot be, I want so much for you to know what we have come to know. Unfortunately, I may write only a few simple words; the rest your own lives must teach you, even as mine taught me.*

*At first, of course, you will grieve bitterly for us, but you will not grieve alone. That is our consolation and it must eventually be yours.*

*Eventually, too, you must come to believe that life is worth the living. Be comforted even now, with the* end of ours slowly approaching, that we know this with a conviction that defeats the executioner!

Your lives must teach you, too, that good cannot really flourish in the midst of evil; the freedom and all the things that go to make up a truly satisfying and worthwhile life, must sometimes be purchased very dearly. Be comforted then that we were serene and understood with the deepest kind of understanding, that civilisation has not as yet progressed to the point where life did not have to be lost for the sake of life; and that we were comforted in the sure knowledge that others would carry on after us.

We wish we might have had the tremendous joy and gratification of living our lives out with you. Your Daddy who is with me in the last momentous hours sends his heart and all the love that is in it for his dearest boys. Always remember that we were innocent and could not wrong our conscience.

We press you close and kiss you with all our strength.

Lovingly,

Daddy and Mummy

★  ★  ★

Fifty-nine-year-old novelist and essayist Virginia Woolf drowned herself on 28 March 1941. She put a large stone in her coat pocket and walked into the River Ouse near her home in Sussex. Her body wasn't found until 18 April.

Virginia Woolf had a history of depression, mental breakdowns and suicide attempts; she was subject to terrible mood swings and, these days, she would be diagnosed as bipolar. She still managed to produce a huge body of work, including *Mrs Dalloway*, *Orlando* and *The Waves*. She wrote this revealing note to her husband, Leonard.

*Dearest,*

*I feel certain I am going mad again. I feel we can't go through another of those terrible times. And I shan't recover this time. I begin to hear voices, and I can't concentrate. So I am doing what seems the best thing to do.*

*You have given me the greatest possible happiness. You have been in every way all that anyone could be. I don't think two people could have been happier 'til this terrible disease came. I can't fight any longer. I know that I am spoiling*

*Virginia Woolf*

your life, that without me you could work. And you will I know. You see I can't even write this properly. I can't read. What I want to say is I owe all the happiness of my life to you. You have been entirely patient with me and incredibly good. I want to say that — everybody knows it. If anybody could have saved me, it would have been you. Everything has gone from me, but the certainty of your goodness. I can't go on spoiling your life any longer.

I don't think two people could have been happier than we have been.

V

\* \* \*

Robert Baden-Powell, also known as B-P, was a Lieutenant-General in the British army, as well as being a writer and the founder of the Scout movement. He wrote *Scouting for Boys* in 1908 and, from then onwards, devoted himself to developing the Scout movement. In his final years, he lived with his wife Olave in Nyeri, Kenya. He died aged 84 on 8 January 1941. He wrote a farewell letter to Scouts everywhere.

*Robert Baden-Powell*

*Dear Scouts*

*If you have ever seen the play* Peter Pan, *you will remember how the pirate chief was always making his dying speech because he was afraid that, possibly, when the time came for him to die, he might not time to get it off his chest. It is much the same with me, and so, although I am not at this moment dying, I shall be doing so one of these days and I want to send you a parting word of goodbye.*

*I have had a most happy life and I want each one of you to have a happy life too. I believe that God put us in this jolly world to be happy and enjoy life. Happiness doesn't come from being rich, nor merely from being successful in your career, nor by self-indulgence. One step towards happiness is to make yourself healthy and strong while you are a boy, so that you can be useful and so you can enjoy life when you are a man. Nature study will show you how full of beautiful and wonderful things God has made for the world to enjoy. Be contented with what you have got and make the best of it. Look on the bright side of things instead of the gloomy one.*

*But the real way to get happiness is by giving*

*out happiness to other people. Try and leave this world a little better than you found it and, when your time comes to die, you can die happy in feeling that, at any rate, you have not wasted your time but have done your best. 'Be Prepared' in this way, to live happy and die happy – stick to your Scout promise always – even after you have ceased to be a boy – and God help you to do it.*

*Your friend,*

*Baden-Powell*

★　　★　　★

Captain Robert Falcon Scott wrote his last letter 'to his widow' on tiny scraps of his journal over a period of days as he and his companions tried to battle their way back from the Pole in sub-zero, blizzard conditions. He wrote while huddled in a tent at the South Pole in 1912; it was minus 70°C, a storm was gathering, and they were 11 miles from the supply camp. Scott had a three-year-old son, Peter, as well as his wife, Kathleen, and it was to them that his thoughts turned as he succumbed to frostbite, malnutrition and exhaustion.

*Captain Robert Falcon Scott*

*To my widow*

Dearest darling – we are in a very tight corner and I have doubts of pulling through. In our short lunch hours, I take advantage of a very small measure of warmth to write letters preparatory to a possible end. The first is naturally to you on whom my thoughts mostly dwell waking or sleeping. If anything happens to me, I shall like you to know how much you have meant to me and that pleasant recollections are with me as I depart. I should like you to take what comfort you can from these facts also.

I shall not have suffered any pain but leave the world fresh from harness and full of good health and vigour. This is dictated already, when provisions come to an end, we simply stop where we are within easy distance of another depot. Therefore, you must not imagine a great tragedy. We are very anxious of course, and have been for weeks but in splendid physical condition and our appetites compensate for all discomfort. The cold is biting and sometimes angering but here again the hot food which drives it forth is so wonderfully enjoyable that we would scarcely be without it.

We have gone down hill a good deal since I wrote the above. Poor Titus Oates has gone. He was in a bad state. The rest of us keep going and imagine we have a chance to get through but the cold weather doesn't let up at all. We are now only 20 miles from a depot but we have very little food or fuel.

Well, dear heart, I want you to take the whole thing very sensibly as I am sure you will. The boy will be your comfort. I had looked forward to helping you to bring him up... it is a satisfaction to feel that he is safe with you. I think both he and you ought to be specially looked after by the country for which, after all, we have given our lives with something of a spirit which makes for example.

I must write a little letter for the boy if time can be found to be read when he grows up. Dearest that you know cherish no sentimental rubbish about re-marriage. When the right man comes to help you in life you ought to be your happy self again.

Dear, it is not easy to write because of the cold... 70 degrees below zero and nothing but the shelter of our tent. You know I have loved you, you know my thoughts must have constantly dwelt on you and, oh dear me, you must know that quite the worst aspect of this situation is the thought that I shall not see you again...

Since writing the above we have got within 11 miles of our depot with one hot meal and two days' cold food and we should have got through but have been held for four days by a frightful storm. I think the best chance has gone. We have decided not to kill ourselves but to fight it to the last for that depot but, in the fighting, there is a painless end so don't worry.

I am anxious for you and the boy's future. Make the boy interested in natural history if you can. It is better than games. They encourage it at some schools. I know you will keep him out in the open air. Try to make him believe in a God, it is comforting. Oh my dear, my dear, what dreams I have had of his future and yet, Oh my girl, I know you will face it stoically – your portrait and the boy's will be found in my breast and the one in the little red Morocco case given by Lady Baxter.

There is a piece of the Union flag I put up at the South Pole in my private kit bag together with Amundsen's black flag and other trifles. Give a small piece of the Union flag to the King and a small piece to Queen Alexandra and keep the rest, a poor trophy for you.

What lots and lots I could tell you of this

*journey. How much better it has been than lounging in comfort at home. What tales you would have for the boy but, oh, what a price to pay. To forfeit the sight of your dear, dear face.*

*Dear you will be good to the old mother. I write her a little line in this book. Also keep in with Ettie and the others. Oh, but you'll put on a strong face for the world, only don't be too proud to accept help for the boy's sake. He ought to have a fine career and do something in the world. I haven't had time to write to Sir Clements. Tell him I thought much of him and never regretted him putting me in command of the* Discovery.

★   ★   ★

Twenty-five-year-old Wilfred Owen was a poet, patriot, soldier and pacifist, and is best known for his war poems written during World War I. When the war broke out, he was teaching English at a language school in Bordeaux, then found himself visiting wounded soldiers in hospitals in France. He was so profoundly affected by these visits that he went back to Britain and signed up for the army. He became a Second Lieutenant in the Artists' Rifles.

*Wilfred Owen*

By January 1917, he found himself stuck in the forward position in the trenches with the scattered pieces of a fellow officer all around him. He had some kind of mini-breakdown and was sent to convalesce in a hospital in Edinburgh where he wrote most of his war poems.

Back in France during 1918, he won the

Military Cross, but he was finally machine-gunned to death on 4 November near Os in one of the last attacks on German lines before the end of the war. Seven days later, the Armistice was signed but he became one of the approximate nine million who lost their lives in this war.

A couple of days before he died, Wilfred wrote this last letter to his mother. He and his fellow soldiers had taken refuge from German shelling in the cellar of a destroyed house. They were all in good spirits because they knew the war was nearly over, and thought they had survived. Wilfred's fate, though, was far from secure.

*Dearest Mother,*

*So thick is the smoke in this cellar that I can hardly see by a candle 12 inches away. And so thick are the inmates that I can hardly write for pokes, nudges and jolts. On my left, the company commander snores on a bench. It is a great life. I am more oblivious than the less, dear mother, of the ghastly glimmering of the guns outside and the hollow crashing of the shells.*

*I hope you are as warm as I am, soothed in your room as I am here. I am certain you could*

*not be visited by a band of friends half so fine
as surround us here. There is no danger down
here, or if any, it will be well over before you
read these lines.*

   *Your loving son,*
   *Wilfred*

     ★   ★   ★

Dr Thomas Hodgkin was the physician who, in 1832, discovered Hodgkin's Disease – cancer which affects the lymph system. He was also one of the earliest defenders of preventative medicine. He died aged 68 on a journey to Jerusalem with his old friend, known as 'the Jewish pope', Moses Montefiore. He was already ill on his departure and he only made it to Jaffa in Palestine (now Tel Aviv) before being taken ill. He died on 4 April in 1866 in the company of a British diplomat. He wrote a last letter to his wife which he dictated to the diplomat Habib Kayat.

*Dearest,*

   *My kind friend Habib Kayat, in whose house
I have been nearly a fortnight, writes a few lines
for me as I cannot hold the pen. I wish in the*

shortest terms to say all that is loving, grateful and affectionate to thee, to thank thee for thy great kindness and to excuse all my deficiencies.

I knowest how intensely I love my brother and his family, but I can only send love and say how much I have thought upon them.

My dear love to all my friends, I lament the little service I have done and I entreat all to – and serve – Lord and Maker.

The two last days at Alexandria knocked me up. The weather was oppressive, I have been in almost ceaseless agony, the delirium, tenemus and gasping have worn me down. Dear Sir Moses was obliged to leave me to go to Jerusalem, but has been boundless in kindness and spared nothing for my relief.

Kayat will give you the particulars, I am grieved at thy continued perplexities. The Lord deliver you out of them.

I don't say there is no chance of some improvement before this is posted but I would not leave thee without a letter. God bless thee, my faith seems tried to a hair's breadth.

Thine most affectionately,
For Thomas Hodgkin

*Epilogue*

Psychotherapist Malcolm Stern believes last letters 'can act as a wonderful gift in that they can be such an affirmation of life'. The value of a last letter is wide ranging. 'It can act as a memoir, add meaning to their existence and also be an opportunity for the person who is writing it to be at their best,' says Stern.

As for the tradition of soldiers writing last letters to their loved ones, this appears to be unofficial. 'Soldiers in World War I were encouraged to fill in the back of their pay books as a form of Will,' says Rod Suddaby, Head of the Department of Documents at the Imperial War Museum, 'and they probably started writing last letters to their relatives when they saw how many casualties there were. But I can't imagine that the army would officially encourage them to write them. It wouldn't be good for morale.'

Suddaby says the pattern that emerges in last letters written during the world wars is a mixture of stating their affection and thanks to the family, comradeship and a philosophical statement about the nature of war. 'They want to help prevent their families bearing the burden of grief,' he says. 'Essentially, letters from both eras are similar in content. Although the language may vary, by the Second World War more sentiment had become popular.'

Last-letter writers, of course, have many different motivations. The soldier, for instance, is writing his letter in the hope that it will never be opened. 'He hopes to hell that he's not going to die,' says psychotherapist Phillip Hodson. 'The last letter in this case has a magical element to it, in that the soldier hopes it will protect him.'

On the other hand, the fatally ill know that they will die, so their last letters are written from a different place inside themselves. 'They are saying "Don't forget me", as well as "These are the things you might want to remember about us",' says Hodson, 'and they also fulfil an important role in the grieving process. As do the soldiers' ones. They prevent the recipient feeling guilt and blame, which is very helpful.'

Suicide notes can be hurtful, funny, kind or simply heartbreaking. It depends on the state of mind of the writer. 'Sometimes, suicidal people have to be angry at the end, because they are, in fact, depressed, and the anger can create the energy to actually perform the act,' says Hodson.

Prisoners about to be executed have many reasons for writing final letters. They may simply want to say sorry to their victims, or profess their ideological conviction, or they may want to show their love and profess their innocence. And, in some cases, they may not have faced up to their guilt and, therefore, they want to express their anger and resentment.

Whatever the circumstances of the writer, a loving last letter can aid the grieving process immeasurably. 'The problem with grief,' says Hodson, 'is that something has happened that is so big that it's impossible to be rational. That can only change over time, but the last letter is a piece of reality that can be referred to, again and again, in a concrete way. It can help with guilt and blame, and so give the recipient their life back. A last letter can be a lifebelt.'

# Permissions Acknowledgements

Sincere and heartfelt acknowledgement to all the parents, partners, girlfriends and relatives who kindly allowed me to use these precious last letters from their loved ones. Thanks to Helen O'Pray, Jane Little, Bridie Spicer, John Hyde, Keith and Robin Butterfield, Leona Arnold, Elaine Cushley, Pat Wallis, George Ireland, Barbara Cookson, Anne and John Hardy, John and Alison Baines, Catherine Hester, Lyulph Lubbock, Eddie Hancock, Roy Hanley, Yvonne Barlow, Anne Jones, Andrew Saffron, Dorothy and Walter Schwarz and Hardev Singh.

Thanks are also due to William Gordon (for letters from World War II Japanese Kamikaze pilots), Fredonia Books (for the Russian letters), www.bbc.co.uk/ww2peopleswar site (for letters from George Cope, Leslie Ford and Herbert Coolum), Grashoff (for German suicide notes which were borrowed from his book *Let Me Finish* published by Headline in 2006), Laura James (for Harriet Parker's letter found on her website and which she extracted from *Twisting In The Wind; The Murderess and the English Press* by

Judith Knelman on University of Toronto Press 1998). Excerpts from Capin Scott's last letter appear by permission of the Scott Polar Research Institute MS1835; BJ

Where it has proved impossible to locate the families and relatives (mostly via the Imperial War Museum) of these letter writers, I would like to say I have tried my best to find them. The Imperial War Museum would be grateful for any information which might help to trace those whose identities or addresses are not currently known.

# *Picture Copyright*

Page 8 Photograph of Neil Downes
© *Manchester Evening News*

Page 29 Photograph of Captain Nicholls
© The Imperial War Museum

Page 32 Photograph of Officer MA Scott
© The Imperial War Musuem

Page 148 Photograph of Zoe Schwarz
© Habie Schwarz

Page 167 Photograph of Patrick H Pearse
© Topfoto

Photographs on pages 177, 179, 183, 187, 191, 195, 199, 201 and 204 © Rex Features

Photographs on pages 193 and 209
© Getty Images

All other photographs reproduced courtesy of the families and friends of those who wrote last letters.